DISTANT BLUE HORIZONS

Journals of a female backpacker aged 48 ¾

SOUTHEAST ASIA

Also by Susanne Spencer

FICTION

A Place of Forgiving

NON-FICTION

Attract Happiness the Natural Way

Know your Self ... Be your Self

DISTANT BLUE HORIZONS

Part 1 – India & Nepal

Part 2 – Thailand & Malaysia

Part 3 - Indonesia

POETRY

Silent Spaces

A Collection of Poems

DISTANT BLUE HORIZONS

Journals of a Female Backpacker aged 48 ¾

SOUTHEAST ASIA

Susanne Spencer

For Jessica

Stay Bold and Brave

CONTENTS

****

Introduction.. 1

INDIA

Starting Out... 7

The Taj Mahal & Agra..............................17

Delhi in Extremis.................................... 21

Sleeper to Gorakphur........................... 33

NEPAL

A Brief Stop in Kathmandu............................ 47

On to Pokhara...................u........................ 51

The Trek... 63

Pokhara after the Trek........................... 87

Back in Kathmandu... 97

THAILAND

Bangkok..111

Ko Samui..119

Unsettled after the Storm.......................................131

Close Connections..141

A Brief Stop in Hat Yai..155

MALAYSIA

Georgetown, Penang..156

INDONESIA

Sumatra..161

Bukit Lawang...165

Jungle Living..169

Lake Toba...181

Bukatinngi... 189

Java.. 197

Pangandaran.. 201

Yogyakarta.. 215

Borobudur... 221

Prambanan & The Ramayana Ballet............. 225

Mount Bromo.. 233

Bali... 237

Ubud.. 241

Lovina Beach.. 251

Senggigi.. 261

Gili Trewangan.. 265

Disillusion in Senggigi.............................. 277

A Brief Return to Ubud.............................. 287

Kuta.. 291

Acknowledgements.................................. 297

A Note from the Author............................. 301

A Request... 303

AUSTRALIA

Sydney.. 305

INTRODUCTION

In 1995 my daughter, then aged 23, was travelling with a Kiwi friend. They had worked their way through Greece and moved on to the Middle East. I was living in Dorset at the time. In September she telephoned me from Egypt and told me about their visit to the Pyramids and how, the following day, their plan was to travel on a felucca down the Nile. I told her how wonderful it all sounded and how I wished I could do something like that. Without missing a beat, she said, 'Well, why don't you!' A caricature image of myself, all five feet one inch of me, carrying a 60 Litre backpack, sprang to mind and so my initial response was to laugh out loud.

I had met up with her the previous month in Crete for a week's holiday. The first surprise came on meeting her, when she picked me up from the airport. My 'little' girl zoomed into sight riding a scooter. I hopped on the back balancing a small case between us and she took me back to where they were staying. I was accommodated in their small room by Julie giving up her bed for me and sleeping on a spare mattress on the floor between the two single beds. It was a taster of a

1

totally carefree life, so different from the one I had known. It was a wonderful, much needed, break. A week later, my return flight was due to depart after midnight from Heraklion and so I had to hang around with many young backpackers as I waited outside the small airport in the heat of the Cretan night.

I had spent the previous four years employed full-time as the Practice Counsellor for a doctors' practice in Dorset. It was in the early days of counselling being accepted and I was the first person to work for them in that capacity. It was also at a time when guidelines for the number of clients you were allowed to see had not been defined by the professional body. I had a caseload of 28 clients, regularly seeing 25 of those each week: far too many. It was very demanding work. I had been considering a different working schedule, perhaps some part-time teaching and a bit less counselling. But backpacking, well that was a step too far. Or so I imagined.

Still, my daughter had planted a seed which very soon became, 'What if …?' I awoke on New Year's Day 1996 with 'Maybe I could …' at the forefront of my mind. In the February I decided to travel to Bristol to an Independent Travellers' Fair. I remember approaching a young woman on one of the stalls there and asking her for some suggestions. I told her I had not seen much of Europe: a couple of holidays in France and one in Spain. Perhaps Italy I thought?

Her response was immediate: 'Well, travel in Europe can be very expensive. What about South-east Asia? Why not take a flight to Bangkok and go from there?'

I hooted with laughter. 'Bangkok! Are you joking?' Visions of a dark and seedy underworld swam before my eyes.

At the beginning of March, I travelled up to London where a seminar was being held, specifically for women travellers. It seemed the idea was growing, taking shape. I decided to put my small cottage on the market. To my surprise, later that month I sold my house in the middle of a very flat housing market. Amazingly, now I had some funds and so there really was nothing in the way.

My first consideration was how I would fare travelling alone. I knew, for certain that none of my friends or colleagues would contemplate such a thing. I did ask but they were all in steady jobs, quite sensible and settled. I considered advertising for a travel companion, although I soon realised that, even if there were someone, I wouldn't know them and so we may not necessarily get on. No, I could see that would not work. I eventually came to the conclusion that travelling alone, I was bound to meet up with other people and, in any case, I was quite used to my own company.

I bought a copy of the Lonely Planet Guide to South-east Asia and began planning my trip. I was determined that I wanted to follow the sun. Whichever countries I was to be travelling through I wanted sunshine, at least most of the time. And so, the plan began to take shape for what was to be an eight month Round the World trip beginning in April.

On April 17th 1996, my daughter drove me to Gatwick airport. She had already suggested what to include in my backpack and so, the evening before we set off, she demonstrated how to go about packing it; an art in itself. As we waited together in the departure lounge at Gatwick, one of the small straps on my new pack snapped. I tried not to see it as a sinister portent. I had not flown much before and, naively, when I realised she had to leave me at the gate, I burst into tears. Yes, beneath the excitement was a good measure of trepidation, to be sure.

On that day, I boarded a plane for Delhi, where there was to be a frightening incident three days after my arrival. I did go on to Bangkok but that was after trekking in Nepal. Later I was to visit Thailand, Malaysia, Indonesia, Bali and from there to Sydney, where I worked as a waitress for the first time. My eight months away was extended to a year. From Australia I travelled on to New Zealand and enjoyed a relaxing final two weeks in Fiji before spending a day and a night in Los Angeles, as my Round the World ticket meant I had to fly back over United States.

What follows is the first part of my Travel Tales and covers, the four and a half months spent travelling through South-east Asia. It is some time ago now, twenty-three years to be precise, when we lived in a world which was, in many ways, less turbulent and dangerous than the present day. There is no doubt in my mind, despite being only one year in a long and varied life, that particular twelve months following the sun turned out to be one of the best years of my life. And so, retracing my steps, this is my journey.

INDIA

STARTING OUT

I am sitting on the edge of the bed, head throbbing. There's a heavy pulsing behind my eyes; an echo of the music we were subjected to until way into the night. It must have turned three before sweet silence descended. The group of Israelis in the room next door certainly pulled out all the stops. Something to do with letting off steam after completing National Service so someone said. I just wish their taste in music went beyond techno. It's unrelenting. I glance over at Marlise in the other bed. She's dead to the world, snoring gently from her joint-induced sleep. She had her first at noon yesterday and, by the time we'd taken a rickshaw to Connaught Place, I couldn't make sense of anything she said.

Our room boasts only a fanlight above the door and a glass panel on the corridor side to relieve the dimness. A skimpy curtain strains to screen us from the constant comings and goings outside in this beehive of a hotel. Mould-green walls soak up the remaining light. The ceiling fan dangles by a thread of wires just above the foot of my bed, creating nightmare visions of mutilation. But given the choice of 'corpus intacto' or keeping cool, there's no contest. From the depths of my slumber I was aware of it whooshing and creaking through the night. Still the room is stuffy. Humid air sucks at my skin, clogging pores, until the whole of my body gasps for breath. This must be the ultimate in budget accommodation.

I reach down by the side of my bed for my water bottle, but it's nearly empty. Just enough to wet my lips, but my throat is sandpaper dry. I make an instant decision to take a quick shower, click on to automatic pilot and stumble towards the bathroom. It's not taken long for me to learn that keeping my eyes half-closed – not difficult in the present circumstances – is the only way to lessen the extreme discomfort in this, my second 'Delhi bathroom experience'. I hurry things along by visualising a plateful of mouth-watering fruit salad and ice-cold banana lassi. Yes, it's working. I'm beginning to drool.

The food in India has been one of the plusses so far, in the few days I've been here. Yesterday evening, with John and Vicky, I dined at Khosla's, a cramped eating-place open to the street. Not much room to move your elbows, but the food was delicious; a spicy Tali with naan bread for the princely sum of twenty rupees – about forty pence. We chatted, and entertained ourselves by watching the world go by in the hustle and bustle of a crowded Main Bazaar. It was delightful.

I had arrived in Delhi at twenty past eleven at night with nowhere to stay, so when Vicky, an Aussie I'd met in the immigration queue at the airport, asked if I wanted to share a room with her and John, a guy she'd met on the plane, I jumped at the offer. She informed me that John had been here before so knew the ropes, as well as a good place to stay. I was so relieved.

We gathered our packs from the carousel and headed out into the night. Clambering on to the only bus in sight, we trundled down to the back seat where there appeared to be more room to spread out. We came under close scrutiny from a group of Indian men seated halfway down the bus. Forget sidelong glances and whispered comments in the British fashion, this was altogether a more open form of communication. They turned to stare, threw in a few loud comments and then finished off with a barely disguised chorus of laughter.

Well, I expect we did look a bizarre trio, but I was too tired to care. And, with my two newfound travel companions, I felt cushioned against whatever India might throw at me. At least one of us knew what he was about and where he was going. How wonderful to meet such a man in just the situation where you needed one. With that thought, I sank back into my seat, closed my eyes and, temporarily at least, chucked the concept of feminism out through the open window of the bus into the stifling heat of the night.

We rattled along drinking in the cool draughts from the wide-open windows. Outside was pitch black and offered up nothing that might signal where we were. Then, without warning, the bus lurched to a halt, jolting us upright in our seats. There appeared to be a great commotion going on outside, although we could see nothing. The driver left his seat, climbed down from the bus and joined in the argument, or so it seemed. A few minutes later, he re-appeared. Our eyes were so trained ahead of us we jumped in unison when two faces appeared at the open window next to John. One of them moved nearer, his head almost making contact with John's arm.

'You come with us. Bus stop now.' He half-turned and pointed to an auto-rickshaw by the side of the road.

Vicky and myself unashamedly left it to John. After all, he was an old hand at this sort of thing.

'No. We go to Janpath. We stay on bus,' he replied.

'Bus not go there. Go different way now.

We looked for confirmation of this timetabling from the driver, but his expression was at the very least inscrutable. I half expected him to shrug his shoulders, but maybe I was just confusing cultures. He turned his back, settled into his seat and lit a cigarette.

'I take you Janpath. Very quick. Good price.'

'But there's three of us. Three people - not enough room.' John pointed to the rickshaw, which would seat a driver and two others with not an inch to spare.

'My friend. He come. Two rickshaw. We go now.' He stood his ground and, grinning victoriously, proceeded to close the deal.

Five minutes later, Vicky and myself were seated in his friend's rickshaw, backpacks on our knees, leaving John to negotiate a price for the journey. I wouldn't have known where to begin!

Sometimes it pays to be an ignorant novice. None of this was wasted however. I was watching John's technique closely and making mental notes for future reference. He was doing really well. I was very impressed. Maybe a few months down the line and I would be, if not exactly a seasoned traveller, at least more accomplished. After all, we all have to start somewhere.

So there we all were. At one o'clock in the morning in, as yet, some unknown quarter of Delhi, price agreed; our two rickshaws lined up side by side, as if at the start of a great chariot race, just waiting for the off. I was wide-awake by now. As the two-stroke engines spluttered into life, I felt a surge of adrenalin as we burst forth into the night once more. To Janpath!

Our little convoy careered along Delhi's deserted streets. Deserted that is except for the strange black shapes here and there, laid out on the wide pavements. It was only when I saw a movement I realised I was witnessing people sleeping, not in the narrow back streets but alongside the broad main roads of the city. I had been told I would be shocked by some of the sights in India, but I realised I needed more time than this, even to begin to take in the differences in culture. I was so unprepared.

I was just wondering how much longer this surreal journey was going to take, when we ground to a halt. I peered round my pack at Vicky, who looked as if she'd been rudely awakened.

'Are we here?' she mumbled.

'I don't know', I answered. 'But I don't understand. There's nothing here. It's absolutely dead.' And it was, literally. We were facing a barricaded street. It was a dead end. A vague feeling of unease gripped my stomach.

John's chariot was still alongside, thank God. This city had certainly brought out the vulnerable female in me and I'd only been here a couple of hours. Our driver jumped down and joined his partner to discuss the next move. I dreaded to think what it might be.

A couple of minutes later it was clear they'd reached a decision, if only by the purposeful way they strode back to their machines. We all charged off again.

'What's happening now?' Vicky drawled casually. This girl was fearless.

'I've no idea, but they're not consulting us on this one.' I replied.

In no time at all we were back at base. At least I guessed it must have been their all-night rickshaw office. It came into view like a shining light in a sea of darkness, though in reality it was just a brightly lit wooden cabin, manned by yet another of their colleagues. Did he have 'The Knowledge' for the inner Delhi area? Perhaps we had been landed with raw recruits who didn't know their Janpath from their Connaught Place.

The six of us clustered in the pool of light from the cabin and, despite my weariness, I could sense the atmosphere was becoming tense. Vicky just shrugged. Definitely a laid-back Aussie. Suddenly, our driver began gesticulating wildly and screamed at John.

'You say Janpath. We go Janpath. No hotel!' He stared at John accusingly. It did occur to me that, as a rickshaw driver, he might have known there were no hotels in Janpath, but perhaps that was pressing logic too far.

'John, can you remember the name of the hotel you stayed in? Maybe that would help,' I ventured. Poor John. I felt quite sorry for him by now. All this responsibility! And now he was being blamed for leading us up a blind alley. This was the downside of male power I mused smugly.

'It was … Christ, it was a few years ago.' To a man, we all held our breath as he concentrated. Even our voluble charioteer kept quiet. 'It was … it was the *Hare Rama*.' A triumphant smile broke through as the frown on John's face dissolved. 'Yes, that's it. The *Hare Rama* in Main Bazaar.' Vicky and myself let out an audible sigh of relief, then shifted our gaze to the driver. It was unusual for him to remain silent for so long. He appeared quite … contained. Then he spoke. Articulating every word very slowly and deliberately.

'Main Bazaar in Paharganj.' And then with a slightly raised tone … 'Paharganj no Janpath.' His lips were clamped tight together now and faint beads of perspiration sparkled on his forehead.

Another great mystery solved. At that precise moment I couldn't help feeling admiration for this little man's restraint throughout the whole fiasco. It seemed as if we'd been cruising the streets of Delhi now for days instead of hours and I realised I'd become quite attached to him in a strange sort of way. I'd heard this could happen whilst travelling: intense friendships formed within short periods of time. Although my affections soon began to pale at the thought of what it might cost us for an unsolicited night-tour, not to mention detour, of Delhi. We clambered aboard again for the last leg. I slumped against my pack but remembered to cross my fingers. About fifteen minutes later we began to slow down.

'This is it. I remember it now.' John's voice wafted on the hot night air. 'We're here.'

I glanced at my watch. It was 2.00am. Two and a half hours after landing at the airport, ten and a half hours after leaving England, we had finally reached our destination.

Now, if I could just summon up enough courage to run the gauntlet of the six or seven cows lumbering across the narrow street, I might reach a place to lay my head for the night. I'd survived Delhi in the dead of night. Things could only get better from now on.

THE TAJ MAHAL AND AGRA

Vicky and I had agreed we could not pass up the chance to visit the Taj Mahal. We both had scheduled so little time in India, it would have to be very soon after our arrival in Delhi. And so, on the Friday morning, despite not having slept well, we were both up and out by 6.20am. We grabbed a couple of fairly stale croissants and some water from the hotel and were escorted to the 'luxury' coach, which in truth looked anything but.

We ended up sitting on a side seat just across from the driver. With minimal padding it was not comfortable at all but I was happy just to be sitting at the front where there was more space. And the view was good. We had been informed that travelling from Delhi to Agra would take about three hours. Instead, from start to finish, including a twenty-five-minute stop, the journey took five and a half hours.

When we arrived in Agra we were escorted off the bus by a 'company guide' and told that they would pay for the train back to Delhi as the late arrival of the bus meant it would not get us back to Delhi until 1.00am. Vicky and I were then taken to book train tickets where we were asked if we would be interested in a 'deal' to earn £1200, or two silk Kashmir carpets, by acting as couriers for them. Needless to say, we declined.

The Taj Mahal was impressive. As it was a Friday, there was no entrance fee and so there were many people there: mostly Indian people milling around, groups of men, couples and many families; the women's colourful saris floating behind them in the slight breeze. There were very few travellers like ourselves that we could see. We strolled along the pathway which runs the length of the reflecting pool with fountains at its centre, until we reached the mausoleum. This gradual approach, it seemed, was no doubt deliberately designed to create an ever-growing appreciation of the building's grandeur: the symmetry of its proportions combined with such intricate carvings in the soft white marble, as one draws nearer to it.

An hour later we were escorted, once more by our guide, to a relatively expensive restaurant for a light vegetarian lunch which I enjoyed. We spent only 80 rupees each. After a trip to Agra Fort and a pre-arranged visit to a marble craft stall, where we were again given the 'big sell' we finally found the train station. Our evening meal was a passable and cheap vegetable cutlet in the station refreshment room. I was so tired I found it almost impossible to keep my eyes open during the train journey home.

The main focus of our trip, which was to see the famous Taj Mahal, had been enjoyable, apart from the lack of organisation and timetabling we agreed. But more confusion awaited us. When the train came to a halt we both stumbled off in search of the main entrance hall at New Delhi station, not far from where we were staying in Main Bazaar. The problem was that no-one had informed us that this station was on the other side of the city. One very obliging young man informed us that for a rickshaw journey to Main Bazaar we should expect to pay about 35 rupees but, despite our protests, the rickshaw drivers would take no less than 50.

On our return we both joined John at the Hare Rama for a drink and a bite to eat. I made my excuses and left at midnight as I had to wash a few smalls and take a shower. I finally fell into bed at 1.15am, dead tired. Before my battered brain ceased to function altogether, I made a mental note to check on my train to Gorakhpur first thing in the morning.

DELHI IN EXTREMIS

I'd planned to stay only three days in Delhi, then travel overland by train and bus to Nepal. Onward booking arrangements, laid out clearly in my Lonely Planet guide, appeared straightforward. No problem! Yet, sometimes, knowing *what* to do, even in the best of circumstances, often proves to be a very different matter from carrying it out. This was Delhi and, for this particular uninitiated traveller, in this colourful city, there were unexpected things yet to be discovered. In this case, a simple procedure, like finding the appropriate entrance to the train station and then locating the booking office to buy a ticket for my onward journey to Nepal was to become a nightmare: a small matter of being dragged off in different directions by people who knew exactly the right way to everywhere.

They were so keen to help, and I was no doubt giving off all the signals of a stranger in a strange place. The upshot was that when I arrived at the recommended destination, it was never the place I wanted to be and there was usually some other helpful soul wanting to get me the 'best deal' available, but strangely, always at an exorbitant price. The

Lonely Planet Guide did its best but somehow, in Delhi, things just did not work out as you might expect.

It took several forays for the penny to drop. There appeared to be an unwritten rule: nobody could bring himself to admit he didn't know the answer to your query. The word 'No' or 'I'm sorry, I have no idea' or just a shake of the head was not part of the language, at least not when directed at gullible travellers. Maybe they did have a sincere desire to help out and any refusal would be impolite or, for them, a loss of face, but it caused such confusion.

I assumed everything was going well that morning at least. I needed to change some money and someone from the Hare Rama suggested I go to the bank at the Imperial Hotel, warning me not to accept more than a twenty-rupee charge for the rickshaw journey. John had advised me always to change any big notes at the beginning of each day, so that I could tender the exact change for any other transactions, especially with the rickshaw men. Once handed over, a note disappeared into their bag and, by the time they shrugged their shoulders to tell you they had no change, it was too late. Small notes were in such short supply that everyone hung on to them. Handled constantly through the years in this way, they have reverted almost to their original state, feeling more like the softest cloth than paper notes.

After a late breakfast I wandered down to the railway station to buy my ticket. I quickly located the reservations office and took my place in the queue outside the building with everyone else. The queue moved fairly quickly and the door soon came into view. Not long now, I thought.

Beside the door, crouching on his haunches, was a policeman. He appeared to be leaning on a rifle and, as I drew level with him, in one swift movement brought it down across my path. My heart started to pound. What had I done? He gestured for me to open my day-pack, peered in and pulled out my camera. Despite the language barrier he made it very clear I was not allowed in and so, distinctly shaken, I had no choice but to return to the hotel.

I quickly realised my mistake. I had been queuing with all the local people because, in my eyes, I was not a tourist but a traveller or backpacker. Perhaps once more naïve and too fine a distinction, because clearly, in theirs, I was simply a foreigner and as such was designated a tourist. I had been standing at the wrong entrance altogether. The tourist booking office was in a completely different part of the station.

I returned later and located the main entrance easily enough. Any thoughts of making progress faded quickly however, when I was stopped by someone who looked like an official. He told me 'advance' bookings were in a different place, so I trotted off behind him only to end up at Adventure Travel. Talk about going round and round in circles! The first tour operator I had asked about train tickets had been one of their agents. They were about to charge me 450 rupees for a train ticket I knew for certain should only be 204 rupees.

By this time all the sleeper trains out of Delhi were full, right up to Wednesday 24th. I had no choice but to accept my fate, which was to stay in Delhi for another three days, if only to learn the lessons life was desperately trying to teach me! As I made my way up to the rooftop restaurant of the Hare Rama that Saturday evening, my plan was to put the day's struggle behind me and relax with a book I'd bought the day before in Connaught Place. What do they say about the best laid plans?

I was sitting on my own at one of the tables, having just eaten and enjoyed a small dish of egg-fried rice, as a change from the fruit craving I'd developed in the stultifying heat of Delhi. It was about 8.00pm and the restaurant was crowded with the usual mix of people, mostly travellers: European, Australian, Israeli, some British and a few Nepalese. There was a buzz of conversation and some music playing: all in all, a very convivial scene.

Suddenly, without any warning, an almighty explosion ripped through the night air. Questions raced around in my head in the space of a few seconds. What on earth could it be? It was certainly nearby, but where exactly? Was it a bomb and, if so, who was responsible? Perhaps facing potential threat, our mind will seek the reassurance of an immediate answer, any answer, as a way to allay fear. In so doing, even the slightest of certainties appear to offer some measure of safety.

It crossed my mind it might be connected with the Israelis. There were so many of them in Delhi, and it must have been only six or seven months earlier that Yitzhak Rabin was assassinated in Jerusalem by a suicide bomber. I tried to quell the tight feeling of panic that gripped my gut, and then rose to my chest. I had never heard a bomb explode before, except on television but it seemed to me that's what it had been.

I had been staying in the *Ajay*, a hotel adjacent to the *Hare Rama*, just across a narrow alleyway. All my belongings were still there. Did it come from there or from this building? It was certainly close by. We all rushed over to the edge of the roof and in the narrow street below there was absolute chaos. People were screaming and shouting and Main Bazaar, usually crowded anyway, was thick with people pushing to see what was going on. It was mayhem. I was relieved to be up above it all.

I was surprised to see a fire engine manoeuvring its way slowly up the narrow street and parting the seething throng in its path. I hadn't expected such efficiency in the tumult of New Delhi. Yet, I should have realised that in certain matters, supposedly because of their history of British influence, Indian procedures could be meticulous. The vehicle was moving past the *Hare Rama* in the direction of the place I'd been staying. I decided it was time to venture down into the street to discover the exact location of the explosion. Maybe I would not be able to get back to my room to retrieve my backpack. At least I carried my money, passport and documents with me at all times, thankfully. I could not replace those.

I reached the entrance of the Hare Rama, which opened on to the alleyway about a hundred metres down from Main Bazaar. Peering out from the top step was like standing on the terraces at a football match before seating was introduced. Standing only five feet one inch tall and claustrophobic to boot, there was no way I was getting down from that step. I managed to catch a guy who I knew worked at the Hare Rama and asked him if he knew what it was and, even more important, where it was.

'It's the hotel next door to the *Ayjay* – an explosion,' he told me, before rushing off to join in the melee. I breathed a sigh of relief, but then my blood ran cold. I had been staying at the *Ayjay* the last two nights. Then it occurred to me it might just have been the other side of the wall to where I'd been sleeping this afternoon. I felt sick, but then my thoughts quickly turned to the people who had been staying at the hotel itself.

Suddenly, I experienced a desperate urge to be with other people, although I knew no-one. Vicky had left that day and, although John was due back briefly this evening, I hadn't yet seen him. Would he be able to make his way back through the crowds? I ran back upstairs and on to the roof. Some people were still hanging over the railing at the edge of the roof. Others were clustered in groups, heads together talking in a desperate fashion. The atmosphere was very tense and somehow expectant. I re-took my seat and looked round. At the table across from me was another woman, food uneaten on her plate.

'Have you been down to look what has happened?' she asked. She spoke with a German accent. 'Did you see anything?'

'No. I couldn't see a thing,' I replied. 'I didn't even try to go out of the hotel. There are just so many people down there. A guy downstairs says it's the hotel just two doors down from here, next to where I've been staying. I think from what he said there might be some people injured, even killed. It's just terrible!'

We introduced ourselves. Her name was Marlise and she was German. In the confusion I forgot I had already checked out of the *Ayjay* because John had told me he was leaving that day. I was hoping to get a room at the *Hare Rama*. John arrived later, around 10.30pm, having made his way via the back streets, Main Bazaar being impassable. Marlise was going to Agra for the day tomorrow and John was leaving Delhi. They both had to be up around 6.00am.

Everyone was feeling unsettled. At first, we decided we would stay up all night, both of us reluctant to be on our own and finding a measure of comfort in being with others in the wake of the explosion. I know I was still feeling very anxious. Eventually, tiredness overcame us and, although it took some grovelling, I persuaded them to let me stay in Marlise's room for the night. I hardly slept at all during the night and woke the following morning thinking I must leave Delhi at once. I was beginning to hate the place.

We went down to the street after breakfast and what met

our eyes was even more horrific than I could have imagined. The road outside of the hotel had been cordoned off, but we were so near to the scene of the blast that we could see everything anyway.

Paharganj is a well-known travellers' area and its main thoroughfare, Main Bazaar, is lined on each side with budget hotels: very basic accommodation at cheap prices. This particular hotel – I didn't know its name – next to the *Ayjay* had just disappeared. Where it once stood there was now a gaping hole in the row of buildings, nothing but rubble below. I looked up, and hanging from a jagged wooden beam by its strap was a backpack. The sight of it was too shocking. It seemed unreal.

Later that day, in Connaught Place with Marlise I saw a newspaper in English that carried a report of the blast: 17 people killed, including travellers and 29 injured. They reported it as a gas explosion, but the feeling on the ground was of a connection with Kashmiri separatists.

In my panic that day, I charged halfway across Delhi to find a bank where I could cash some U.S. dollar travellers' cheques. I arrived back, after a frustrating journey by auto-rickshaw, only to discover that the guy in reception, who promised to arrange the ticket for me, was intending to rip me off in a big way. I also got a bad rate of exchange. A hard lesson in how it's always better to give yourself some time to think and respond rather than react on the spur of the moment.

Later that evening, back in the restaurant at the Hare Rama, we listened to a young Israeli describing how, after enquiring about his wife who was due to meet him in Delhi at any time, he'd been called to identify a silver necklace which he thought may have belonged to her. Thankfully, it wasn't hers. But it did belong to someone. He described to us the scene of carnage at the hospital. Above all he said he would never forget the smell of burning flesh. I found myself near to tears as he spoke.

Later that evening, around 11.00pm (6.30pm British time), I phoned my son to say I was O.K. just in case they had heard anything. I don't know why I was surprised to hear the incident had been reported on the National Television News. They had phoned the British Embassy to check the names of people involved when they heard the news report. It was good to speak to him, albeit briefly. What a shock for them. I'd only been away three days!

By this time, my panic was subsiding. Why should another

bomb, if that's what it was, be planted around the same place? I was becoming more philosophical! I reverted to my original plan of leaving Delhi by train. I couldn't wait to leave now but wondered what the next leg of my trip might bring.

SLEEPER TO GORAKPHUR

I remember as a child I loved to walk on narrow walls – not too high of course. And there was always a hand there to hold if I needed it. 'Whatever you do don't look down. Keep your head up and look straight ahead.' That's what they told me.

All those years ago I was a good little girl – at least most of the time – and so I did as I was told. I learnt how to maintain my balance and I never did fall. After such a close call in Delhi, I decided this was to be my strategy for the next few weeks, at least when the going got tough, especially as, on this occasion, there would be nobody to hold my hand. Maybe that's what got me through.

At least now I had a vision to work towards. Last night in the restaurant at the *Hare Rama*, I chatted to Steve from Leeds who was just back from Nepal. He was with an attractive Nepalese guy, named Depindra, who painted a delightful picture of the Annapurna Sanctuary Trek. I listened appreciatively as he talked, whilst munching my way through egg-fried rice and vegetables. As I was due to leave Delhi the next day to head for Nepal, I decided the trek to

Annapurna Base Camp or ABC would now be my vision for the future, which I intended to hold in my mind's eye, especially when negotiating any 'narrow walls'.

The following morning, I started preparing for the off as soon as I woke. I managed to get everything into my backpack yet again which, at this early stage in my travelling career, still seemed like a minor miracle. I was becoming accustomed to this simple, uncluttered existence – carrying my home on my back. Depindra had agreed to meet me in the restaurant. I went up around one but there was no sign of him, so I read for a while.

He arrived at four o'clock. 'Sorry, I've been sleeping,' he said. There was that smile again and for a second or two my concentration slipped. He passed on some useful information about arriving in Kathmandu and suggested one or two places I might stay. He also told me that to do the ABC trek, I would first need to travel from Kathmandu to Pokhara, possibly a seven-hour journey by bus. Once there, I would need to obtain a trekking permit as soon as possible.

I had read about Pokhara, a lush valley nestled beneath the snow-crested Annapurna Massif 125 miles west of Kathmandu; Pokhara itself beside the still waters of Phewa Lake. It would be indeed a seductive place in which to relax after the stresses of India, but Depindra recommended that I make the trek first as we were nearing the end of April. The pre-monsoon season was nearly upon us and the mountain pathways would soon be very wet, making walking more difficult. I thanked him for all his help, he flashed me a lovely smile, wished me 'Namaste' and was gone. Nepal became even more appealing after meeting him.

Just another two hours now in Delhi. I went to say goodbye to Marlise and then came back and ordered some chow mein. I felt I should eat something before I set off but I didn't enjoy it at all. I was beginning to feel anxious about the train journey and I just could not relax. I had a sense of really being on my own for the first time, on this next leg of my journey and, probably, in quite different circumstances than I had thus far experienced in the week since I left England. Was it only a week? So much had happened already, including the small matter of being a hop and a skip away from a bomb blast. Still, I was unscathed, at least physically.

It was dark when I set off for the train station about 6.15pm. Even though my pack was heavy, I decided I could just about manage to walk there but unfortunately, I was only half way along Main Bazaar when it started to rain. I was aware that this would be my last sight of Delhi and, even though there had been stressful moments and disturbing sights in the last seven days, there had also been colour, vibrancy and eccentricity. I understood why so many people loved India, despite possibly experiencing a love-hate relationship with Delhi in the first instance. I was truly sad, therefore, that a final goodbye along this route I had come to know was not to be. The darkness and pouring rain conspired against me. It meant too that most of the stallholders along Main Bazaar were hidden from view. Still, fewer distractions made it easier to keep my internal eye fixed on Annapurna Base Camp. With this in mind I trudged on.

The concourse at New Delhi railway station was teeming with people. I'd given myself plenty of time, anticipating the degree of difficulty I might have in simply trying to locate the appropriate platform. I had learnt that nothing was as you might expect in this crazy city. I was looking for the Delhi to Gorakphur train, due out at seven o'clock. Amazingly, I found it with fifteen minutes to spare. I walked along the platform, past one, two, three, even more carriages, staring into the brightly lit compartments until I found mine. I looked down at the ticket I was clutching in my hand. No mistake, it was this carriage.

But then a strange kind of paralysis crept over me. I seemed to be rooted to the spot. Un-strapping my pack and dropping it to the floor I stood there surveying the scene. I looked down once more at the ticket in my hand. Seat number 35 I read. Yes, this was my ticket! I recalled the moment I bought it and the exact price— 204 rupees. But seat number 35— what a joke! Rising hysteria rapidly changed to panic. I struggled hard to visualise ABC, but the more I tried to focus, the more the sparkling image dissolved and slid away, leaving only stark reality before my eyes.

The carriage was literally jam-packed with people— all of them, or at least 99.9% of them, men. Of course, what was I expecting— the 8.30am to Paddington, with my own seat, a table and a buffet car! Not until that moment did I fully feel my 'lone female traveller' status.

I can't get on, I just can't, I'll not be able to breathe. Then*: but I have to get on, I can't turn back, I've nowhere else to go.* Then: *what did you expect you fool, you are in Delhi? This is reality, not some travellers' haven!*

And with that thought reality hit me like a smack across the face. I realised what an ignorant Westerner I was with such narrow experiences of the world. 'Well, this trip is about rectifying at least some of that,' I told myself— out loud. I realised I was talking to myself. At that moment I must have looked like a gibbering idiot, because someone— an English-speaking Indian man— swept by me.

'Are you getting on? I'll take that for you,' he said. I opened my mouth to answer him but, by then, he had already picked up my pack and made for the steps of the carriage.

'What's your seat number?' he shouted over the din on the platform which only now broke into my consciousness.

'Thirty-five,' I yelled after him, realising I had better follow him if only to retrieve my backpack. At least I'd made some kind of connection after spending the last ten minutes swirling around in a sea of my own dark imaginings.

I could never have been prepared for what met my eyes. I had seen through the window how full the carriage was and anticipated the kind of crowded carriage in the tube at rush hour. This scenario required a shift in perception. From the moment I set foot in the carriage I had to clamber over people, trying hard not to stand on anyone, which was difficult, as every available inch of floor space was taken up with bodies.

The seats were, of course, full to overflowing and, as I glanced up, I noticed pairs of disembodied legs swinging from the berths above the seats – well, it was a sleeper train! People were even sitting on the floor inside the toilets, wedging open the doors. I kept my eyes fixed on my dark green backpack bobbing along behind my saviour. Rather than slinging it over his shoulder, he was dragging it along the floor behind him. Once or twice I winced as it delivered one or two nasty blows to those unfortunate enough to be in its path.

'Here we are,' he shouted, about halfway along the carriage. He sat down and cleared a space next to him for me to take a seat. I didn't check but I suspect at least two people must have slid off the end of the bench seat the moment we sat down.

I sat with my pack wedged between my knees, breathed as much of a sigh of relief as was possible in the circumstances and looked up. To my amazement and delight sitting opposite were two fellow travellers. They turned out to be Chris and Julie, a young couple from Manchester, my own hometown. What a relief! I would have some travel companions once again I thought … a little too prematurely.

Just a few minutes after 7.00pm, as the engine started up and lots of whistles were blown, another Caucasian joined us in the already overstuffed compartment. Pushing his way through the crowd he made straight for the open window, clearly unhappy that no seat was available. But no matter how much he protested, there still wasn't an inch to spare and, by then, we were moving. By his accent I guessed he was American. He seemed lost in his own world: head down, unwilling to acknowledge anyone. His strategy seemed to work because, after a few minutes of his swaying and complaining, someone stood and offered him a space. He slumped into the seat by the window.

I chatted to Chris and Julie a little and to my Indian friend sitting next to me. During our conversation, he took great pleasure in informing me that one day in the near future India would become a very powerful nation because of the sheer volume of her population.

Despite being squeezed into my space, the journey wasn't unpleasant and I began to relax, although it crossed my mind that a journey to the loo might prove a little awkward to negotiate. I had been suffering from a touch of 'Delhi belly' – not helped by all the fruit I'd been eating to slake my constant thirst - and the journey to Gorakphur was likely to take about ten hours after all.

After a time, the brakes squealed and we stopped at a station. There was much hustle and bustle on the platform, where a man shouting, 'Chai, chai,' was selling steaming cups of tea and passing them through the bars of the train's open windows. Someone in the compartment bought food as well. I could smell ginger, coriander, and maybe cumin, spicing the hot night air.

I didn't see exactly what happened next, but learned later that someone had decided to spit out of the open window, perhaps not uncommon in certain situations in Indian culture. However, he had leaned across the American, who may inadvertently have been a recipient of some of the flying spittle, no doubt borne on the back draft of the train's forward motion. Objecting strongly to this unwanted gift he, quite forcefully, pushed the Indian away. A scuffle broke out and, a few seconds later, they were fighting.

But very soon, the fight was unfair: three Indians who, though admittedly small, set against the one American; himself slightly built, wearing only a vest tee shirt and by now, looking vulnerable. They were all yelling and one of his opponents was raining down punches on him from above. The American was still seated, but cowering in the corner by the window, nose bleeding, arms above his head attempting to protect himself.

It was frightening to witness and, as the tension mounted, I half-expected that at any moment the whole carriage might erupt and turn on him. I looked across at the young English guy sitting opposite me. He must have been six feet tall but he clearly didn't want to get involved. He didn't move a muscle. Neither did anyone else. I knew I couldn't sit there much longer watching this guy being beaten to a pulp.

Instinctively, at an opportune moment I stood up, grabbed the chief aggressor, who had his back to me, round the middle and dragged him away, somehow managing to sit back down in my seat in the process. He wheeled round, his arm raised, no doubt to punch the person who had dared to intervene but, on seeing a female, his clenched fist instantaneously transformed itself into a pointing finger. He shouted something, which of course I didn't understand, although I could take a guess at the basic content, all the time wagging his forefinger an inch from my nose.

I held my breath, but remained seated, unmoved by his threats, even though inside I was petrified. Luckily, it did the trick, somehow creating enough of a lull in the attack to stop it completely. After hurling a few insults at the American, and muttering, both to themselves and between each other, the three of them sat down and the journey resumed as before. The only difference being that the American didn't utter another word, only sat there nursing his bloody nose and rubbing his bruises throughout the remainder of the journey.

About eleven thirty, some of the passengers, having left the train, I clambered up on to the top berth, dragging my pack along with me, thankful to have it there to hold on to at that moment. I curled into a foetal position, which in any case, happened to be the only possible option in attempting to sleep, as one third of my berth was taken up by three people perched happily on the bunk at my feet, legs swinging, for most of the night.

We arrived in Gorakphur at six-thirty in the morning. I opened my eyes to the sight of Julie throwing up all over the carriage, after which she crumpled to the floor. We managed to revive her and an Indian guy very thoughtfully gave her some water from his bottle. Chris decided he would take her to the nearest hospital to be checked out, which was likely to take hours.

Until I was out of India, and because of recent events, I just did not want to be completely on my own, which only left as a potential travel companion, the reluctant American, whose name I learned at that point was Daniel. Normally sensitive to when I'm not wanted, at that moment, survival was uppermost in my mind, at least until I regained some equilibrium. The signals he gave out were hardly warm and welcoming, unlike most of the fellow travellers I had met so far. There was never any mention of my part in his 'rescue' and I wasn't sure how much he had been aware of it at the time. Still, whether he appreciated my company or not I was determined to stick to him like glue.

We took the bus from Gorakphur to Sunauli, on the Nepali border where I had to obtain an entry visa. A little girl of about ten, elbows resting on a low wall stared at me through enormous black eyes as I queued for my visa. I smiled at her and she smiled back at me. It was a big, friendly smile. I saw it as a positive omen and began to feel better about my situation. I was at least now in Nepal and one step nearer to my vision.

I tagged along while Daniel looked up someone whose name he'd been given in his search for dope. While he did the deal, we ate something and then a little later set off to catch the night bus to Kathmandu. Daniel, happy now with his stash, smoked most of the time, sometimes communicative, sometimes not, probably not appreciating my constant presence, but I didn't care. After the incident on the train, I just needed to be with someone who could communicate with me in the event of an emergency, even though when he did speak he couldn't manage to string a sensible sentence together. I realised how much we cling to any fragment of the familiar when feeling isolated or threatened by the unknown.

Yet I was O.K. with that and knew in time it would pass. And so as accidental, if somewhat wary, travel buddies, we chose to sit together on the bus.

By this time, I was beginning to feel I couldn't trust anyone. The Indian travel guys in charge of the bus wanted to put my pack on the roof, but I insisted on keeping it with me, although they weren't happy about it. I dozed on and off throughout the night but I never took my hands of my pack - my home - propped beside me in the aisle of the bus. At various other stages, the bus stopped and other items of luggage were loaded on to the roof and at one point, in the middle of the night, several long wooden crates came sliding along the central aisle of the bus. In my half-asleep state I automatically lifted my pack to accommodate them.

The bus park was a few miles out of town and we were dropped off at the ungodly hour of 4.30am. It was deserted, pitch black and freezing cold. I was tired and my body was aching and the only form of transport available to us to get into Kathmandu was a taxi. The worst was yet to come. When we both stumbled out of the back seat of the taxi on arriving in Kathmandu, the seat of my cotton trousers was wet through. I looked across at Daniel's blank face but thought better of it. Don't even go there, I told myself.

We booked into the first place we found that was open and paid half each for the room, not speaking at all by now, all pretence at companionship gone. Daniel collapsed on one of the beds. I took off my pack and lay down on the other. I slept for two hours until 7.00 am then made my escape in search of a decent place to stay, leaving Daniel lying in a stupor, snoring away.

At the door, I turned and took one last look at him before I left and spotted a bed bug nestling by his left ear. Relieved I hadn't seen it earlier, I made my escape. The air was warm and welcoming. People were already at work sweeping their little piece of street front. Kathmandu was stirring, coming to life.

NEPAL

A BRIEF STOP IN KATHMANDU

I was dragging my feet around the early morning streets of Kathmandu in search of the *Valentine Guesthouse*. The name was appealing enough but, like the day of the same name, I was aware it might prove to be a cause for delight or a dismal disappointment.

As soon as I stepped foot inside I could see that the reality was somewhere in-between. It was plain and simple: practical, without any pretensions to impress the weary traveller, which by then I most certainly was. However, it was clean, and an unexpected bonus came in the shape of Bahrat, the manager. He was so welcoming and helpful I almost cried with relief.

I washed away some of my weariness in the shower, changed my clothes and went out to explore Kathmandu.

Since leaving Dehli I had been suffering from a tummy bug, which I hoped wouldn't develop into anything more serious. I did feel very weak though as I wandered around the streets of Kathmandu, by now teeming with people. I stopped to quench my thirst in an outdoor restaurant and started chatting to Amy, a young English girl, who later showed me where the Thai airline office was located. I had to make booking my onward flight a priority. She invited me to dinner with herself and a few friends, but in my present delicate condition the company of others for longer than a few minutes was more than I could face.

The plan was to leave for Pokhara the following day and so Bahrat kindly offered to organise purchasing a ticket for me. He also knew of a tailor who would sew the strap on my backpack, which had snapped at the beginning of my trip. Bahrat was rapidly elevating himself to the status of ministering angel and when I offered to pay him extra for his support he would not hear of it. I found the tailor easily enough in a street not far from the hotel and that evening I packed my, now very sturdy, backpack with confidence, wrote some letters and was in bed by 9.30pm.

Sleep was elusive, probably because I was too hot inside my sleeping bag, but I was mostly using it for protection as I had spotted another bed bug earlier on. Just as I was on the verge of sleep a pesky mosquito decided to begin dive-bombing manoeuvres, which did not help at all. The creatures must have been hiding as I settled down for the night and so I had not bothered to rig up my net; always a mistake.

The following morning, I rolled out of bed at five thirty, bleary eyed. Neither was there any breakfast to look forward to at that ungodly hour, only water. I imagined that even Bahrat, accommodating as he was, drew the line at dawn farewells. Still, I was eager to begin this next leg of the journey after everything I'd heard about Pokhara and the trek and so off I set with a spring in my step.

ON TO POKHARA

It was 6.00am when I left the still sleeping *Valentine Guesthouse* behind and set out once more into the streets of Kathmandu, along the way passing only the odd person sweeping the front of stalls and doorways. At least it was cool at this time in the morning. I'd estimated it would take about twenty minutes to walk to the bus stop, not far at all. But halfway there, my feet began to drag and no doubt because I was tired, my pack seemed much heavier than usual. Once at the bus stop it was taken from me and slung onto the roof of the little single-decker.

The bus, painted red and white, had on its side big blue letters which proclaimed, 'PEACE & HAPPY TRAVELS'. It must be prophetic I thought and then, raising my eyes to the jumble of packs on the roof, I could not suppress a smile. What a beautiful sight. A sure sign that I would, from now on, be in the company of other travellers. It crossed my mind that if no collective noun existed for a large heap of backpacks I would suggest a 'comfort.' That's how it seemed to me at that early stage in my travels.

I took a seat in the bus and one of the Nepalese travel

guys asked my name. He smiled, but the slight frown revealed the extent of his pity as he said, 'Sue – but that's such a little name!' Now, like most 'Susans' or 'Susannes', of my generation at least, it had taken some time to become a 'Sue', almost four decades in fact, but this exchange caused me to reconsider. I really believe it was a defining moment for me … in the name area at least.

I was soon joined by Deanna, an American, aged twenty-nine and also travelling en route to Pokhara. But she was planning to do the Annapurna Circuit trek, which meant she would be getting off the bus before we reached Pokhara. We chatted a little and snoozed a lot and then, just as my stomach began to growl, the bus drew in to a breakfast stop. We climbed down from the bus and sat together beneath an awning drinking, what in South East Asia is referred to as, 'plain' tea, that is, tea without milk. It was still very early in the day and so eating fruit and sharing some bread was a perfect antidote for my hunger pangs.

The long and winding road from Kathmandu to Pokhara clings to side of a mountain. The road twists and turns, following a deep gorge high above the Treshuli River, passing through small villages along the way. Not very long after setting off from our breakfast stop, I peered through the window and spotted a bus similar to our own, lying rusty and

52

mangled at the bottom of a precipitous drop to one side of the road: a sinister portent or simply an old accident whose evidence remained because of where it lay? However, I would later learn this particular road was indeed known to be dangerous and that some drivers were less than competent. But in that precise moment I suppose I was simply content, due to a combination of blissful ignorance, the physical sensation of a full stomach, agreeable company and scenery which absorbed every ounce of my attention.

Through our window great swathes of emerald green paddy fields dotted with figures stooping to their work came into view. Clusters of squealing children played as they washed in the river, dark skin glistening in the morning sun, whilst brightly coloured boulders nearby displayed their newly washed clothes. After my stressful time in India I sensed this little country would offer a completely different experience.

It was two thirty before we arrived in Pokhara. I knew I would probably be here at least for a few days, as it would take some time to organise my trip to Annapurna Base Camp. Several people I'd spoken with had nothing but praise for Pokhara, as an attractive and relaxing place and so, to make the most of my time here, I wanted to find a good place to stay.

But, as with all arrivals at unfamiliar places, without any prior recommendation I had absolutely no idea in which direction to head. My problem was solved in what would become typical of most of the decision making throughout my travels. Setting off from the bus station, just by chance, I found myself sharing a taxi with three British people who were on their way to Butterfly Lodge, a place that had been recommended to them. Perfect timing and with such an appealing name I didn't hesitate.

I was allocated a room, with attached shower. It was stark but clean and looked out on to an attractive courtyard edged with flowers. I unpacked and then stepped outside to take my first look at Pokhara and to locate somewhere I could eat that evening.

Pokhara is known as 'The Jewel in the Himalaya' for good reason. A place of outstanding natural beauty, with the magnificent Annapurna range as a backdrop and the serenity of Lake Phewa in the valley, its appeal to weary travellers is as magnetic today as when it lay on the trade route between India and China. But at this point I knew little of Pokhara and had yet to discover its charms. In Delhi, Depindra's enthusiasm about Annapurna Base Camp was my inspiration for choosing this particular trek. However, it seemed he neglected to tell me anything much about

Pokhara itself. I knew it was a good place to relax and that it was from here I would be setting off on the trek. It was almost the end of April and, more than once, I had been told that ideal trekking conditions would soon be adversely affected because of the rains and so, on my arrival, securing my trekking permit was at the forefront of my mind. I decided it would have to be on my return, after the trek, that I would experience for myself what Pokhara had to offer.

I strolled along the main street, a mix of small budget hotels, restaurants, bars and souvenir shops and then ventured into some of the narrower lanes to get a feel for the place. There were travellers like myself everywhere I looked, although usually in pairs or small groups. It was vibrant and peaceful at one and the same time. Perfect after the stresses of India and only ten days after leaving England I'd managed to land in what seemed to me to be a perfect haven.

I arrived at the *Pyramid Restaurant* at 7.30pm, hoping they would be willing to change a $20 Travellers' Cheque to enable me to pay for the meal. Thankfully, they agreed and so I ordered vegetable lasagne and what turned out to be rather a large beer. Before it arrived, I moved table to sit next to a young woman from Sidney who had come to Pokhara to do some rafting. I was hungry, maybe craving a square meal after my prolonged fruit diet in India and so, for me, the lasagne was both satisfying and delicious. My stomach, on the other hand, having shrunk somewhat in the last week, would perhaps have got on better with an accompanying glass of water. Maybe it was the Australian influence and perhaps joining her in a beer was simply a desire to celebrate, happy not to dine solo on my first evening in this magical place. Whatever, I returned to Butterfly Lodge, sated with good food and conversation. It was hot and stuffy in my room but, after sorting out some accounts, I rigged up my mosquito net and read by torchlight.

On my way out at eight thirty the following morning I encountered two women heading out into Pokhara. They were on their way to have breakfast at *Boomerang*, a restaurant down by the side of Lake Phewa and invited me to join them. Ten minutes later we were seated at a table in the most enchanting garden setting overlooking the still waters of the lake. I ordered fruit salad and curd, which was delicious and the three of us chatted easily.

I discovered Claudia was a primary school teacher and lived in a village in the mountains in the German speaking part of Switzerland. She was forty-eight, the same age as me and her birthday the day after mine. Nicole was her daughter and lived in Zurich. Claudia had come out to Nepal for a holiday and to meet up with Nicole who was travelling with friends. We exchanged addresses and she said I was welcome to visit her in Switzerland. I had met up with many people in what seemed such a long time, but was in fact only eleven days, since leaving home. Yet this meeting with Claudia seemed to me to be the first genuine connection I had made and, with it, came a sense of reassurance that somehow all would be well going forward on this adventure of mine.

Meanwhile, I was still on a quest to meet other people who, like myself, were aiming to begin the Annapurna Base Camp trek as soon as possible. Back at Butterfly Lodge I spoke with two French Canadian women who had recently returned from the ABC trek. They had hired a porter but, at $6 a day, if I was away for fourteen days, an extra £50 or more would burn a serious hole in my budget. Making up a small group with others was still my preferred option. Still, they told me where to go if all else failed and I should decide to hire someone.

That evening I tried another restaurant, the *Tibetan Garden*, which looked appealing and bumped into Nicole and Claudia for a second time. After all, Pokhara was a small place and we clearly had similar tastes in restaurants. Nicole left to see a friend and I spent the evening once more with Claudia. I enjoyed a plate of vegetable mo-mo and, again, found Claudia a most interesting companion. On our way home, we called in at *The Pyramid* for a coffee. Later, back in my room at Butterfly Lodge I was kept awake for most of the night by the constant heavy rainfall and, because of it, my concern about getting organised for the trek.

The next morning, I decided I would try to change my flight date to give me more time in Nepal. As a designated Round the World trip I had had to book eight flights in advance, the dates of which could be changed where necessary. Unfortunately, despite several attempts, no-one answered my calls. By this time, it was late morning and, in complete contrast to Pokhara's relaxing ambience, I realised I had been running around in a kind of frenzied panic and understandably, had achieved very little. I took a deep breath and resolved to try to slow down, even to stop and re-think my approach.

Almost on automatic pilot I wandered down to *Boomerang*. It was cloudy after the rain and maybe in keeping with my introspection I found myself eventually at the same peaceful spot by the lake. A veil of mist hung like gossamer above the water of the lake. I sipped my coffee and gazed at the scene as the heat of the sun broke through. When I looked around an attractive young man was sitting at the next table. I wondered if he might be doing the ABC trek. My answer came an hour later when I saw him again in the place I went to arrange my trekking permit. There was a short queue and, just a minute after I arrived, he came in and took the place behind me. 'Which trek are you planning to do,' I asked, in a voice inflected with what I hoped was a casual tone. 'Oh, hi,' came back an Aussie drawl. 'Gary,' he said holding out a hand. 'I'm doing the Annapurna Circuit. I've been in Pokhara longer than I'd planned. It's so easy here, isn't it?' I nodded and smiled in response, feeling a bit of a fraud.

After lunch I tried Thai airlines again with no success and at 4.00pm hired a bike to go back to pick up my permit and, as seemed to be the way of things in Pokhara, saw Gary once again as I was cycling back. Without so much as a wobble I waved gaily. After returning the bike, I did some more shopping: bought another bum bag, a long sleeved top and a map of the Annapurna treks.

After a quick shower I went out to eat, this time in the *Maya Restaurant*, where I ate vegetable curry and rice and later, my second large beer of the trip, which I took my time over whilst reading a book. I looked up from the page at one point and spotted Chris and Julie from the Gorakphur train, Julie clearly now much recovered. We exchanged stories since our time together on the train and they asked if I wanted to join them later at the *Blues Bar*, where they had won quite a few beers playing pool. I appreciated their offer but, as I was walking home, it started to pour with rain and so I decided to stay inside. I didn't want to risk getting drenched again and my one large beer had been sufficient for the evening. I clambered under my mosquito net, read for a while and fell into a deep sleep.

The French Canadians at *Butterfly Lodge* had hired a porter and given me a contact name of Emma at the *Yeti Guest House*. However, despite a couple of attempts to locate her there, I had been unsuccessful. The following day I tried once more, but by 12.00 noon she had not returned. It was the last day of April and the rains were already here. I made a snap decision to hire a porter anyhow and get off tomorrow. The Chetri sisters, who ran the *Yeti Guest House*, told me then that Khem, my Nepalese guide, would arrive at *Butterfly Lodge* tomorrow around 6.45am.

I checked on equipment hire and decided to go for a Gore-tex jacket and trousers to combat the cold during my overnight stay at the Base Camp. Next stop was the bank to draw out money for the trek, some of which I used to buy gloves, a hat and a backpack cover because of the rains. Now things were moving forward. At 5.00pm, having swapped addresses with Claudia and Nicole and packed some of my things, I sat for a while on the porch feeling cool and relaxed, but excited about what the next week would bring. The air was fresh now after yet another downpour lasting about forty-five minutes. I just prayed I hadn't left it too late.

THE TREK

Day 1

There was a power black-out last night because of the storm and Govinda kindly lent me a candle. In the end though I decided to put up the mosquito net and read by the light of my trusty Maglite torch as I was being dive bombed from every angle. I woke about 5.50am still a little tired but then did the final sorting out of things to leave and things to take. I was concerned that Khem would have too much weight to carry, even though the sisters had assured me that less than 10 kilos would be fine. I had packed my sleeping bag and so one thing I decided I would not need was my very-much-used bed-sheet. I left it behind to be washed.

Khem arrived at *Butterfly Lodge* early, at 6.50am. It struck me that he had a look of some of the Indians I had encountered in Delhi. He was only about five feet seven, slightly built and softly spoken. I gave him my 60 litre backpack, now almost half-emptied. 'Would it be O.K? Not too heavy?' He smiled and said, 'Of course. No problem.' My small day pack, which I usually carried across my front, I now slung on to my back and we set off to the *Yeti Guest House* where the taxi was to pick us up and take us to the bus park.

Khem and I shared a taxi to Birethanti with Anton, an Australian and Mike from San Francisco. They were going to Ghandrung, taking the quicker route to A.B.C. but I wanted to go to Ghorepani. We arrived at 8.30am. Our very first steps on the trek were over the suspension foot-bridge, which hangs from cables above the River Modi at Birethanti. After about thirty minutes along the river valley bottom we began a climb upwards which seemed to go on for ever. Much of the ascent was made up of actual steps. I began to believe this was maybe the stairway to heaven and, just at the point when I thought I couldn't lift my foot to climb one more step, we finally arrived at Ulleri at about 3.30pm.

Khem disappeared soon after our arrival, no doubt to spend time with people he knew at the lodge. He hadn't spoken very much during the day despite my attempts to make conversation. That was fine by me as I prefer not to talk too much on long walks and the silence was not at all awkward. After getting my breath back and taking a shower, I ate a delicious meal of vegetable curry, potatoes and rice in the restaurant of the *Annapurna View Point Lodge*. The only other people staying there were two guys, one from Liverpool and one from north London and a girl from Buckinghamshire.

Our paths crossed again briefly in the restaurant, where later we ate by the light of a dodgy looking kerosene lamp as there was no other lighting in the Lodge. They were heading off early just as I imagined Khem and myself would be doing. By 9.00pm. I was exhausted and crawled into my sleeping bag in the pitch black of my small room, hoping it wouldn't take too long before my muscles would become accustomed to a full day's trek.

Day 2

I woke at 5.30am after a restless night, partly because I was too hot in my sleeping bag. At six o'clock I stepped outside to see Annapurna in the far distance, clear and shining white against the dawn sky. After a cup of tea, we were away by 7.00am. Khem, perhaps realising how exhausted I was last night, had promised me it would be easier today and it was. We walked very slowly and without speaking as if, by unspoken agreement, we both concluded it was far too early to talk. Only the sweet sound of Khem's whistling occasionally broke the silence. The trail took us through lush, green landscape alongside the river, close by a number of magnificent waterfalls and past large swathes of pink, red and white rhododendrons, the Nepali national flower. In

65

contrast to the heat and exertion of yesterday, it was cool, fresh and moist and only a gradual climb. The sunshine dappled through the leaves in places. At times, it was so peaceful that walking in this way was like a meditation.

From time to time, bells would announce the arrival of donkey trains both going up and down the trail. Their heads were adorned with brightly coloured harnesses, on which several bells sat and jingled with every movement they made. Strapped to their backs were what seemed to be cruelly heavy loads and yet I soon realised that some of the Nepalese men accompanying them carried their own burdens. One of them I saw carrying a large fridge, which was on his back but, unbelievably, strapped round his forehead to take the weight. How they didn't break their necks I don't know.

We stopped for a delicious breakfast of pancakes at the *Hungry Eye Lodge* in Banthanti at 9.00am and then carried on slowly to Ghorepani arriving around noon. Just as Khem had told me, today was a much shorter trek, in all about five hours. On arrival at *Snow View Lodge* I used the extra time to wash a couple of tee-shirts and some smalls and then I took a shower. After a morning walking through brilliant sunshine, as if the gods were playing games, around two o'clock it started to rain and began to feel quite chilly inside the lodge. Khem reassured me that Suan would light the fire later on and that's exactly what happened. By then an American couple, a Danish couple and three Australians, two male and one female, whose names I learnt later, had arrived at *Snow View* and we all ended up hanging our washing to dry around the fire, which created a cosy and surprisingly homely atmosphere. I read for a while and later in the evening chatted with the American and Danish couples.

Staying at Ghorepani, the accepted ritual was to rise even earlier than usual, to allow time to climb to the top of Poon Hill by 5.30am in order to witness the sun rise over the Annapurna mountain range and so this is what we all planned to do. It was a clear night with a full moon and so all the better for venturing outside before daybreak. The trouble was that during the night, I had suffered from an attack of the runs and had to make my way outside on two occasions. Still I woke at 4.45am, imagining, for a few seconds, that the shrill tones of my alarm clock were part of a dream.

Khem and myself were the first to set out at 5.00am. The others followed soon after and quickly overtook us, as it didn't take long before I was dragging my heels, climbing so slowly up, what seemed to be, an almost perpendicular ascent. What with the lack of sleep and probably weak from the night-time trips, it almost did me in. As a precaution, I chose to stop for a short break about half way up, the prefect excuse to take some photos as the sun was glowing red behind the mountains.

Finally, triumphant and just in time, I reached the top of Poon Hill at 5.35am, the last of our 'party' to arrive. At that moment the sun was rising from behind the mountain tops, illuminating the whole of the Annapurna range with its clear, shining light. It was indeed an amazing spectacle; the wonder of it almost biblical and, perhaps for most people, a 'once in a lifetime' experience. I understood then why almost everyone trekking to ABC makes the effort to see it from this vantage point.

We arrived back at *Snow View* at 7.00am in time for breakfast. An hour later, Khem and myself set off to walk to Tadapani, uphill again into quite dizzying heights. The views were breath-taking. At the first peak we passed a group of French guys and a lone woman. As we approached the group one of the men, a big guy, reminded me of someone I once knew; something to do with the shape of his head and the way his hair was cut. I experienced a fleeting pang of sadness and yearning.

About fifteen minutes later, the scenery changed dramatically when we descended into a densely forested jungle-like area; a stark and immediate contrast and, as if to intensify the gloom, Khem informed me that this area was known to be dangerous. Not long ago, a Japanese tourist had been attacked here and his money stolen he told me, seemingly unaware of the effect his news might have on me. I felt a sudden lurch within my already queasy stomach.

I had foolishly imagined that, after leaving India, I would never again experience any danger. I had become used to Khem covering ground quickly, often opening up a distance between us but, from that moment, I made sure I stayed closely behind him as he blithely strode on through the forest. Noises up ahead made my heart beat faster until, in plain sight, a group of half a dozen Nepalese men, carrying their heavy burdens, approached and then passed by. Perhaps I was fooling myself but I felt a little easier knowing there were more than just the two of us in that forbidding place. Later, as we climbed up the other side and out of the forest we spotted the French group at the bottom of the valley. I breathed more easily then.

We arrived in Tadapani at 1.00pm. I checked out a few of the lodges and decided on the *Hotel Grand View*, at the furthest end of the village. Khem too, gave it his seal of approval. I decided I would take a shower which helped to ease my sore feet. After three days of constant walking enclosed in my boots, it was no surprise they were complaining and so I changed into sandals to give them a breather.

Outside of the lodge was a cold-water pump. I was in the middle of cleaning my teeth just beside it, when a very attractive Italian guy engaged me in conversation. Under the circumstances, it was a little awkward to begin with but, once I was able to answer him, we exchanged the usual news about where we came from and where we were going. By then he was joined by an equally attractive, slightly smaller Nepalese guy, by the name of Tara. Our paths were crossing literally as they had already been up to A.B.C. Christian told me it was amazing.

The evening was spent in the dining room. Coincidentally, another Tara, a twenty-six-year-old young woman from California with braided hair, was travelling with Shane and Sheldon, both Australians. They had met up in Kathmandu. We met briefly at *Snow View Lodge* in Ghorepani when I had assumed they were all Australian. They too had a Nepalese guide by the name of Khalu. Christian, the Italian, joined us for dinner and so the three Nepalese guides, Khem, Tara and Khalu sat together with us as the rain began its usual evening downpour, accompanied for the first time by a storm – crashing thunder and sheet lightning.

As we all sat around a large table waiting for our food to be served and listening to the rain drumming on the roof, our hosts brought in a kerosene lamp to light the room. Soon there were moths circling. There were large windows on two sides of the small room and, as a back drop to the storm, a full moon hung in the sky creating the perfect dramatic setting. As if on cue Christian, charming and eloquent, began the story of *Siddartha*, as a way of illustrating how he had come to make his decision to go travelling.

He had worked as a food manager in an Italian restaurant in Hong Kong and tried every way possible to get promoted, but without success. Even more disconcerting, for a time, he believed he may have contracted HIV from his girlfriend. It turned out not to be, but all of this prompted him to give up his job and travel for two months in Nepal. Just two months, but it was clear this was a big move for him. I would be away for at least eight months and my 'story' untold thus far, was certainly longer.

Day 3

The following morning around eight o'clock, we bade farewell to everyone and left Tadapani. We would be heading back to

Kathmandu after the trek and so there was every possibility we would see Christian and Tara—whom I had secretly christened *The Beautiful One*, to distinguish him from Tara, the American girl—back there. So too, I realised we would no doubt encounter Tara, Shane and Sheldon once again up ahead. Along the way, I met up with Katrine a German woman who also had a guide with her. We walked along together for a while and chatted. She told me she lived in New Zealand and after Nepal she would be going to Tibet, and then travelling to India where she wanted to do a yoga course. It wasn't long before we were overtaken by the two Australians and the American girl. Khem took the opportunity to steam ahead with Khalu, their guide.

Yet again, the walk was very different from the previous day. Most of it was along a ridge, precariously narrow in places and overlooking a deep and fertile valley, with the Modi Khola river flowing along the bottom. People were working on the land, which was intricately terraced and planted with corn and potato crops. At the end of one of the terraces, a woman stood, alone and softly singing, whilst scything hay in rhythmical time to her song.

We eventually arrived at Chomrong, a delightful spot, about 2.00pm. Khem tried to persuade me to stay at a lodge where he knew people but by then I was becoming more confident, not needing to rely on him so much. Besides, at the very bottom of the steps, I had spotted a very attractive terrace, with tables and chairs and lots of potted plants creating a splash of colour. Perfect. I headed down there and was shown a room which was only 25 rupees. The toilet and shower were spotless and so we booked in there. It turned out to be the best place so far and the food was delicious.

Shane, Sheldon and Tara were already there and soon Katrine arrived. I met two young English girls, Emma and Nicola, both of whom I discovered had been on my flight from Gatwick to Delhi. They were staying at *Chomrong Lodge* for two days, having given up on ABC, as Emma had done her ankles in and Nicola had asthma. Not surprisingly, up to now, they had found it hard going. I silently congratulated myself for my resilience thus far. I also met Karin, a Swedish girl and Rosarie, an Irish girl who kindly gave me a telephone number for when I arrived in Sydney. I was beginning to appreciate just how important the connections were that you made whilst travelling.

The evening was lively, with lots of talk and laughter, altogether very convivial. Tara told me a little about the island of Ko Tao off the coast of Thailand. I went off to bed well fed but happy around 9.30pm and slept reasonably well, interrupted only once to venture out on the, by now, sporadic but still lingering, night-time trips.

Day 4

I woke at 6.15am and fifteen minutes later I had packed my bag. Breakfast was muesli, warm milk and apple and then a slice of toast. I felt far too full. My bill was almost double what it had been before. So much for being enticed by colourful pot plants! Perhaps I should have listened to Khem. Nevertheless, I had met new people and enjoyed their company. At least I managed to wangle a free bottle of water from their filter machine. I put some iodine in it for the first time and, although it tasted foul, I still drank it by two o'clock when we arrived at Doban.

Doban, in stark contrast with Chomrong, was deserted and appeared to be a dismal place, but we had been walking solidly for six hours and the skies looked decidedly grey. At 3.45pm it began the predictable late afternoon downpour. All the same, I wished we had pushed on just that bit further today. Khem assured me that it would take us only five and a half hours to reach (MBC) Machhepuchhre Base Camp, where we planned to stay tomorrow night.

I met up with two couples, one French and one Polish but, just as I anticipated on arrival, compared to the previous evening, this one turned out to be sedate and lacking in atmosphere, somehow matching the weather and the surroundings. Like a thwarted child, I felt only disappointment.

Day 5

With Karin and Rosarie I set off from Doban just after 7.00am. It was dry, but dull until the sun came out and, owing to the previous day's deluge, the rocks were slippery beneath our feet. We reached Himalaya around eight and stopped for breakfast. Shane, Sheldon and Tara had stayed there the previous night. Khem had gone ahead a little way as usual, but I felt fine as Karin and Rosarie walked just ahead of me. Once or twice, having lost sight of them, I went the wrong way, but not very far. It became quite hard going as we climbed higher with each step.

We finally reached MBC at twelve thirty and stopped for some lunch. There was quite a group of us by this time — Shane, Sheldon, Tara, Karin, Rosarie, Paul from Sydney, Colin from Newcastle, myself, Khem and Khalu. These were the people I would be spending time with at Annapurna Base Camp. We were now on the last leg of our trek. I felt a mixture of excitement and trepidation as we were entering unfamiliar terrain yet again. From Doban we had witnessed a marked change and no doubt would again before reaching ABC.

We all headed off at 1.15pm. At first the going wasn't too bad and I was up in front but, pretty soon, it became more difficult, especially at one point where we had to cross a massive avalanche of ice spreading out at a steep angle over part of the mountainside. The trick, we were told, was to climb as high as possible before attempting to cross. Khem fashioned a long bamboo stick for me, which I used as a walking pole. Even so, I slipped down a few times before finally managing it. Once safely across, I learned from one of the others that, had we attempted the crossing in the wrong place, any one of us might have disappeared through the ice and been lost forever. To this day I don't know if prior knowledge of this gruesome detail would have literally stopped me in my tracks. Still, safely on the other side of this hidden threat, I could now breathe a very large sigh of relief. What other hidden dangers lay ahead I wondered.

The landscape had changed dramatically now. Great expanses of frozen snow lay before us reminiscent of the kind of scenery in the Arctic. The air at this higher altitude was noticeably much thinner, making breathing more difficult. It was only possible to move very slowly, trudging onwards in the footsteps of those who had gone before. It did not take long before I was trailing well behind all the others and thankful that, at least over this terrain, which was quite desolate, Khem had stayed by my side.

I remember the moment when, convinced I would be last to arrive I turned, only to spot a lone figure just behind me. An open face, rimless glasses and shoulder length, fair hair, secured with a broad head band. In his right hand he carried a stout walking pole; something I realised would have come in handy, especially over the avalanche. With what breath we could muster we introduced ourselves. He was Wilco, a Dutch man and, at that serendipitous moment, a welcome and reassuring presence. Like all the others, he was much younger than I was, but was hampered because he had a problem with his feet and so could only walk relatively slowly.

At this high altitude, approaching 4,000 metres, the air was getting progressively thinner, making any conversation impossible. At the start of the trek, with Khem, I couldn't speak because of the extreme physical exertion. Now approaching ABC with Wilco, I was struck dumb for a completely different reason. In what seemed like an alien landscape, the mist was rolling in behind us obscuring everything around. We could see little ahead of us and were forced to keep our eyes trained on the ground, with only footsteps in the snow as our signpost to ABC.

I struggled to suppress the very real anxiety that we might not make it: that in this eerie atmosphere, the freezing mist would envelop us entirely before we reached our goal. Wilco and myself moved forward together, one step at a time, breathless and wordless. I cannot speak for him but, for my part at least, I was so thankful he was there.

Finally, out of the mist appeared a cluster of small, stone buildings on a rise about a hundred metres ahead of us. We had finally arrived at Annapurna Base Camp and were welcomed by the others. It was 3.00pm on the sixth day after setting off from Birethanti. It was also freezing cold. Not surprising, as we were now at an altitude of 4,120 metres. The very first thing I did was to change out of my wet clothing and then add more layers including the silk thermals I'd bought just for this occasion before setting off. In the absence of water, I creamed the sweat off my face. The rest of me, including my hair, which for practicality had been shorn, would have to be left.

I was sharing a room with Karin and Rosarie. Soon after our arrival we all moved into the dining room and sat around a big table. A couple of paraffin heaters created a welcoming and cosy atmosphere. In addition to those we had come to know as we climbed towards ABC, already there was an Italian as well as Ted, an American from Boston, who had been teaching English in Kathmandu for two and a half years on a volunteer program. He was such a pleasant guy, extremely polite as is the way with many Americans. He also spoke perfect Nepalese.

The evening turned out to be very convivial. We were all ravenously hungry, no doubt due to the extreme exercise and the air on the mountains. I ate dahl bat, which by now had become an acquired favourite of mine, along with half a plate of chips. Perhaps because the altitude had finally got to me I developed a slight headache at one point in the evening, which Kahlu magically dispatched by means of a skilful head and shoulder massage. Khem and Khalu rounded off the evening in time honoured fashion by teaching us all a Nepali song.

At 10.00pm, Rosarie, Karin and myself were about to retire for the night when we encountered a Russian woman outside our room. She explained that she had just left a Russian party who were climbing Annapurna and was planning to set off down the mountain alone with just a flashlight. We managed to persuade her that it would be far too dangerous at this time of night and alone. She ended up sleeping in our room with Karin and myself. Rosarie slept next door with the Australians and Wilco, the Dutch guy.

I was warm in my sleeping bag but found it difficult to get off to sleep. For the first time I had to wear the woolly hat I'd purchased in Pokhara and it was itchy on my scalp. I took it off at one point but the air was so freezing cold it made my head hurt. I reckoned an itchy scalp was a small price to pay to stop my brain from freezing over.

As arranged the previous evening, Sheldon woke us up at five in the morning so we could take photographs of the mountain at dawn. The scenery was absolutely breath-taking. I could see why it was called Annapurna Sanctuary. What we were unable to grasp on arrival the previous day, when everything was shrouded in mist, was the sheer grandeur and magnificence of the place. The base camp was surrounded on all sides by the mountains and so, to photograph them all necessitated turning full circle. Even as I was taking them though, I was aware that individual photographs of these magnificent peaks could amount only to a suggestion of what we were experiencing by being there.

I decided, along with the others, to rest a day at ABC before attempting the descent. It was very hot and I was tired after my broken sleep of the previous night. For a while I just lay on a bench in the sun and relaxed or chatted to one or two people. We spent another enjoyable evening playing cards and eating rather too much. That night I shared a room again with Rosarie and Karin and slept soundly.

Day 9 – The Descent

Due to a long-standing habit of not wanting to assume my presence is welcome unless invited, I was reluctant to tag along when my room-mates set off in the morning. I followed shortly after at around 8.00am. I felt somewhat anxious about finding my way but I needn't have worried. As I had done on my approach to ABC, I followed in the footsteps of those who had gone before me as they were still fresh in the snow. I caught up with Rosarie and Karin and together we picked our way over the dreaded glacier. It seemed less daunting than on the previous occasion.

We stopped briefly at MBC for a rest and to buy some toilet rolls and then we forged ahead. There was some talk of getting to Chomrong but, because it was already 2.30pm when we reached Bamboo, the general consensus was that we stay there. That meant that I was able to partake in the luxury of a 'hot bucket' shower, after which I changed my tee shirt and my underwear. After sleeping in so many layers of clothing at ABC, it was wonderful to feel so clean again.

The rest of the evening was spent playing cards. Paul taught me how to play 'arsehole' and, despite my history of opting out of card games, I could not refuse to play on this occasion. The evening meal included a delicious rice pudding sprinkled with cocoa powder and washed down with half a glass of beer. I shared a room with American Tara at Bamboo. Before turning in, Paul joined us and we all shared a smoke. Well into my forty eighth year, and this was only the second occasion in my life where I had partaken of a spliff. Needless to say, I slept very well.

Day 10

The following morning setting off at 7.40am, I was the second to head out after Wilco, my Dutch friend with bad feet. I soon passed him and walked on my own for some time. It was so peaceful. Crickets were chorusing and a multitude of birds were singing and calling in the forest. Tara caught up with me after a while and we walked together all the way to Chomrong. The last leg was demanding with steps up and seemingly on forever. We rested and had lunch there and then set off again for Gandruk.

The trek was through a beautiful valley but rather than along the valley bottom it was down one side and then a fairly steep and lengthy climb up the other. Rosarie had joined us by this time, having earlier said farewell to Karin, who had set off to visit the hot springs at Tadopani. We were not able to talk so much as this part of the trek was gruelling. The only way I was able to keep going was by literally concentrating on each step I took and not thinking beyond that. By the time we reached Gandruk at 4.00pm we had been walking for over eight hours. I was beyond tired and my body was so stiff that, even after a shower, my legs and knees were really hurting.

On the plus side, the lodge at Gandruk, the *Sangrila*, was so welcoming; clean and bright with all the finishing touches. There were flowers, even in the loo, as well as those bursting from the tubs on the terrace. Wilco announced he had a problem with his pack which was coming apart at the seams and I was delighted to be able to produce my emergency sewing kit and mend it for him. We all stayed out on the terrace chatting until it became quite dark.

Just before we turned in, a large group of Nepalis arrived

and took all the ground floor rooms. Apart from our guides, it was the first time I'd actually seen any Nepalese people in the lodges I'd stayed at. I shared a room with Rosarie and, before settling down for the night, we had a burst of hysterics as I took it upon myself to catch and eject a spider of frighteningly giant proportions from our little room. Physically exhausted, but peaceful and content, I soon fell into a deep sleep.

Day 11

When I awoke the next day, I was relieved to discover the overall stiffness in my body had eased. Despite this, my left knee was still very sore. I soon fell behind all the others. Khalu had told us that this last leg would take about four hours, half our normal daily trekking time and so, with this in mind, and not wanting to get left behind, I pressed on. For me, it was the most challenging day of the whole trek even though it was the shortest in duration. The scenery was once more just amazing as we walked through a beautiful river valley. Although, as with previous days, it was often difficult to survey and appreciate it fully, as it would have been so easy to lose concentration and balance.

We finally reached Birithanti at mid-day, at the exact spot from which Khem and myself had set out ten days before, only now I was a member of a group. I realised that in striking out, admittedly with Khem, I had finally found the group I had been seeking in Pokhara.

We had some lunch then walked on and climbed up to the road. There were eight of us including myself but, as yet, no Wilco. We hung around for twenty minutes until he appeared on the other side of the bridge. A cheer went up. It was a poignant moment for me. The solidarity of our little group was touching, not to mention Wilco having been a memorable part of my arrival at ABC, as he was now in the final moments of the trek.

Shane, Sheldon, Tara and Khalu shared one taxi for 200/- and Paul, Rosarie, Khem Wilco and myself shared the other for 450/-. The ride back to Pokhara was a bit hair-raising or perhaps, having been on foot for the past ten days, we had forgotten the state of the Nepalese roads and their driving habits. We finally made it back to Pokhara at 3.30pm.

My first stop, along with Khem, was the *Yeti Guest House*, where I went inside to sort out the payment. I was greeted by the Chetri sisters. One of them asked Khem if he would go to buy a Coke for her. While he was away she informed me that, during our time trekking, Khem's father had died. I was very upset and felt guilty that I had taken him away from his home when perhaps his father had been ill. He had said nothing of this to me. I asked did she want me to stay while she gave him the bad news. She said, 'No' quite firmly. Khem then carried my pack back to *Butterfly Lodge*. I was allocated another room, picked up the things I had left behind and then went out to get some shampoo. On my way back, I called in at the *Yeti,* but she hadn't told him at all.

'He will find out when he arrives home,' she told me, 'that is how it is done.' And then she told me that Khem would have to fast for thirteen days. Poor Khem. What a terrible situation to have to come home to.

POKHARA AFTER THE TREK

After leaving the Chetri sisters at the Yeti, I returned to *Butterfly Lodge* to rest. I was exhausted and still experiencing the shock and sadness of Khem's news. We had all arranged to meet up at *Hare's Chai House* that evening. Around 7.30pm I wandered up to *The Pleasure Home* to meet the others, accompanied by Rosarie. We had been told by Tara that it was a very appealing place with a great view over the lake, as indeed it was. Together, we all walked back into the centre to meet Wilco at the *Maya* pub. I ate a very generous portion of vegetable moussaka, which was delicious but sat rather too heavily in my stomach. We spent the next few hours recounting tales from the last ten days. It was very pleasant and comforting somehow. I left at 11.00pm and walked back to *Butterfly Lodge* in the dark. Another power cut!

Despite the stuffiness in the room I fell into a deep sleep and woke at 7.30am feeling very low. To distract myself I decided to wash all the clothes in my pack. Everything, that is, apart from my yellow tee-shirt, which was beyond repair; filthy and blood stained from the leech on my back.

At 8.30am, perhaps seeking solace, I set off for one of my favourite spots by the lake, *Boomerang*, and ate mixed fruit salad and muesli, a dish I'd been craving whilst trekking. After breakfast, I attempted to work out my finances. I calculated I'd spent only a couple of pounds more a week than I'd budgeted for initially, so that wasn't too bad. I would cut back a little during the remainder of my time in Pokhara I decided. On my way to the *Pleasure Home* to meet Tara, I stopped at the wonderfully named *Comfortably Numb Guest House* and discovered I could get a room with shower for 100 rupees. I could stay there and wallow in my depression without feeling bad about it. I did try to work out why I was feeling so down and tearful. I concluded it was partly being alone again after being with the group, but most likely the result of a very rushed phone call with Paul the previous evening, which cost me over 1,000 rupees. We had only five minutes in which to speak. Neither had he been able to give me an address where I could contact Julie. I realised I was missing my family.

On arrival at the *Pleasure Home* I confessed to Tara how I was feeling and was surprised to discover she too had felt the same way. I had assumed this confident young American woman would somehow be inured to such things. I made a mental note not to make such hasty assumptions in future and, as a result of our little chat, I decided to move in later that day.

So, there I was at 3.00pm, freshly laundered clothes in my pack, walking up to the *Pleasure Home*, where I joined Tara and Sheldon on the balcony. Later on, we went down for a coffee and met up with the two Kiwi girls, Kathy and Kim and Rachel, a friend of Shane's. I was so happy to be there, especially when I thought how I might have been sitting in a room on my own, feeling sorry for myself.

That evening, I walked round to *Hare's Chai House* and sat with Kathy and Kim. Kathy gave me her mum's address for when I arrived in New Zealand. Later on, Sheldon joined us and then Tara and Shane. We all left around 10.00pm. My room was cool and airy and, despite the constant barking of a dog as I was falling asleep, I slept well. I was looking forward to spending time at the *Pleasure Home*, which so far, was living up to its name.

The following day was Sunday. I woke at 8.00am and went downstairs for breakfast: mixed fruit curd, which was delicious. I wrote up my journal and then walked into the centre. I made some enquiries about getting my camera film developed and then headed off to *Ganja Restaurant* for lunch, where I met Nicky an Australian girl who worked as an editor in a publishing firm. Before leaving I wrote out some postcards, although apparently my first batch had not arrived as yet.

Back at *The Pleasure Home* I changed into shorts in the hope of exposing my legs to some sunshine, before settling down to read for a while. Not a good move as it brought on the pre-monsoon rain. At 5.00pm, just after Tara and Sheldon returned from the pictures, I set off into Pokhara centre. I bumped into Karin and her sister and then Kathy and Kim and the American woman. When I picked up my photos, I realised I had a roll of film from India missing. It occurred to me I might have left it in the bag they lent me at Butterfly Lodge and so resolved to go back and check the following day. I spoke with Steph back home, who gave me the fax number for *The Drunken Duck* and so I decided I would write to them, rather than risk another frustrating and expensive telephone call.

In the evening Tara went off to visit Kahlu again and so I went to *Hare's* alone. As it turned out, I would have preferred to stay on my own. A woman at the next table engaged me in conversation. But rather than it being two- way, I found myself doing almost all of the listening. She had been the victim of an armed robbery in Indonesia. She described a catalogue of quite terrible incidents. Relieved to make my escape, I was back home by 9.30pm.

Despite the bedtime horror story, I slept well and the following morning, feeling a little low and in the mood to write, I walked into Pokhara centre. Despite spending time with most of the trekking group again, I needed contact, albeit one-way, with family and people I knew well. I wrote out a long fax to Paul, asking for an address for Julie and then wrote a letter to a friend of mine. By the time I had eaten breakfast and finished writing I felt much better.

I called in at *Butterfly Lodge* only to be very disappointed that no-one had found my roll of film. I had lost the few photos I had of India. By the time I strolled back it was one o'clock and very hot. I changed into my shorts and sunbathed on the balcony until Tara returned from her shopping spree.

At 4.30pm I showered and went downstairs for a coffee. Tara was there with an Israeli guy and a German. They all went up later for a smoke. I stayed behind, ate a pancake and read my book. I realised that perhaps because of the difference in our ages, and our inclinations, given a choice, Tara would always prefer to be with someone other than myself. That didn't matter so much. We walked together into town at seven and met up with Emily, another American and

Em, a young Englishwoman staying at the *Pleasure Home*. We all ate at *Ganja*. I had Aloo Palak, an Indian dish of potatoes and spinach, which was delicious. Walking back, we were spotted by the Israeli friend of Tara's and went to join them in the *Pyramid* for a coffee. We strolled back around eleven and I left Tara with Guido at the gate.

I woke at eight the following morning and, perhaps after having enjoyed the physical exertions of the trek, felt inspired to do some of my stretches for the first time since I've been away. Next, it was down for some breakfast. Afterwards, I wrote in my journal and then, for the first time, ventured on to the roof with the two Emilys to watch Tara practising her yoga.

After a slightly different lunch of an egg, tomato and onion toastie, I got talking to a Nepali man who runs an astrology centre and decided I might call in to see him later on. Tara and I walked into the centre to check on faxes. There were none. Then she showed me the place where she had had her overalls made. I liked hers so much I decided I would have pair too; a bit rash really, but the material was an attractive bright green seersucker cotton and would cost only six pounds. To pay for them I cashed my last £20 Travellers' Cheque.

Later, we walked to *Teatime* to eat, a little early at 6.30pm, where I saw Karin and her sister Lisa. I made tentative arrangements to travel to Kathmandu with Karin, possibly on 18th May, which would be a Saturday. We wandered back at 10.00pm and much later Emily, and then Sheldon and Diana, joined us on the balcony. Tara left to start her packing. She would be leaving in the morning.

I was half unconscious as Tara left at six thirty the following morning. I woke at 8.00am, did some washing and then went to settle up Tara's bill. She had left me 150 rupees but actually owed another 170. Luckily, I was not going to be held responsible for making up the difference.

I had breakfast at *Elegant View* and asked the waiter if someone had posted my cards, given that no-one at home had received any as yet. He was very concerned and said he would ask everyone there for me. It was only when speaking with Karin and Lisa, I realised it was actually *Boomerang* where I had handed them in. Luckily, I managed to find the waiter I had handed them to, who swore blind he had posted them.

Back at *Pleasure Home* I sorted a few of my belongings ready for packing and then left for *Teatime* where I ate with a New Zealand woman and an Israeli woman. I arrived back early, about eight just as Sheldon and Diana were going out for the evening and, by 9.30pm, I was in bed reading. Outside, there appeared to be quite a raucous celebration taking place, with people singing, cheering and banging drums. I was still awake when I heard Sheldon arriving back at midnight. I was relieved not to be completely alone up here.

Stretches again this morning, encouraged by Tara's yoga perhaps. Then it was off to collect my overalls, which may well be too hot for Thailand, so I may post them home along with my sleeping bag. Coming back, I saw the astrologer again and stopped to eat some breakfast with him. Then, no doubt under the influence of the stars, I went back to his place and agreed to have my chart drawn up ... I would live to regret it!

I met Karin and Sheldon for lunch and we booked our ticket to Kathmandu for tomorrow. It would be a very early start. Back in my room at just turned 4.00pm I was sitting in near darkness. An hour earlier, a violent storm had started and was still rumbling away. With no electricity at all, I decided to lie on the bed and rest and must have fallen asleep for a short time. Shortly after waking at 5.00pm, I walked into Pokhara to check if I had received any faxes. I discovered that all the roads were flooded and so was thankful I had changed into my boots.

At the fax place I was delighted to have received a fax from Julie but then joy turned to disappointment when I saw that the second page was ripped in half and so the last page of the message was lost. Disappointment turned to anger and frustration as I realised how much I needed to hear everything she had wanted to tell me.

Things went rapidly downhill then. No doubt because of my own neediness at that point, my brain went to mush. I resorted to the telephone to make contact and paid far too much once again. To top it all I went to pick up my chart from the astrologer. I agreed to pay more than I had budgeted for and realised that, in my haste, I had given him the wrong time of birth. The reading was O.K. but nothing special and nothing I had not previously known.

The whole day turned out to be a disaster from start to finish. It taught me always to think things through before agreeing to anything, but mainly to trust in myself, to discover my own answers and not rely over much, or even at all, on other people— especially on the stars! I told myself that from now on, I would wait for things to unfold and not believe I have to know in advance. Suitably self-chastened I packed most of my things before going to bed.

BACK IN KATHMANDU

Awake at 4.45am, up fifteen minutes later and then I was away from *Pleasure Home* by 5.40am. Back on the road, I walked into Pokhara. The streets were deserted, apart from the odd person throwing water to settle the dust and then sweeping outside their house or shop. I reached the 'bus stop' before six o'clock. A procession of orange robed monks filed past; two or three dogs began chasing each other, barking loudly.

It got to 6.05am and I knew then that the astrologer was not coming. The night before, he had said he would bring me my chart. He promised he would be there at 6.00am. Karin arrived at 6.15am and the bus five minutes later. We climbed into the bus, our packs were put on top and we left by 6.30am. He never showed. What a fool I am, I thought to myself. Well, if I am truly to learn a lesson the harder it hits me the better.

The journey to Kathmandu was not too bad. It was quite cold for the first forty-five minutes as everywhere outside was shrouded in mist. As we came out of it however, it became increasingly hotter. The driver, possibly self-taught, hadn't yet discovered how to use his gears. He applied the brakes so frequently I thought they may just wear out before we reached Kathmandu.

On arrival, the bus dropped us near the G.P.O. at 2.15pm. Unfortunately, they had closed fifteen minutes earlier – clearly early closing on a Friday. Karin was hoping to pick up some mail from Poste Restante and I too thought I may have received a letter. We were both disappointed.

We then took a cycle rickshaw up to Thamel, although we could hardly see a thing along the way, as we both had big packs balanced on our knees. We visited *Pumpernickel Bakery,* where Karin was hoping to pick up a note from Rosarie. Whilst we were there Kathy, one of the Kiwi girls walked in and told us they had just moved to a guest house opposite. It was only 100 rupees for a double – cheaper than Pokhara. We went with her and got a room, which was fine, with shower and toilet just a little way down the corridor.

We dumped our things, had a bite to eat then strolled around Kathmandu, in and out of shops and eventually down to Durbar Square, where we sat on the steps and watched the world go by. I felt much more comfortable in Kathmandu this time around, perhaps partly because I was with Karin.

Back at the hotel we showered and around 8.20pm set out to eat. Kim and Kathy were going to the *Roadhouse*, but we were tired and so continued on to *Green Leaves*, where we listened to a Nepali 'combo' playing a dozen variations on *Rosana pere re*; all this accompanied by a resident barking dog, a black cat with a painful limp and a waiter who appeared to be in a constant trance. It was magic!

On Saturday morning we went to *Pumpernickel* for breakfast and then spent a couple of hours wandering around the shops and headed towards Freak Street. There we spotted Shane, Sheldon and Tara, who had been on yet another spending spree. She was struggling whether to go back home after visiting Thailand, instead of going to India as she had planned.

In the evening a large group of us went to listen to some Blues music at *Spam's Space*. This was the 'pub' owned by a British guy who Depindra in Delhi had told me about. Tara's German friend, Axel, passed round a smoke; this being probably only the third time I had ever indulged, it affected me badly as it was very strong. About thirty minutes later, I began to feel sick and came out in a cold sweat. I knew I had to get out of there. Luckily, Tara took me home, holding me gently by the elbow, otherwise I reckon I would definitely have fainted, if not worse. By the time we arrived back at the guest house it had passed off. Nevertheless, I was really frightened. Yet another lesson!

The following day Karin and I had breakfast at *Pumpernickel* and were joined by a British guy, originally from Leicester but living in Edinburgh. He had met Karin on the trek when she left the group heading for the hot springs at Tadopani. In the evening we met him again for a meal of pumpkin pie and baked potatoes, which was good but left me feeling a little bloated. The evening was O.K. but somehow a little stilted. He told us he was an artist and was probably nearer to my age than Karin's. To me his conversation came over as a little 'forced', perhaps because I had grown used to hanging out with young people.

The following morning, we had breakfast and then set off for the Thai Embassy by cycle rickshaw to sort out our visas for Thailand. We were forced to stop for fifteen minutes to let the King go by in his motorcade. The rickshaw man found it impossible to cycle up a hill at one point and so Karin and I disembarked and walked alongside him for a while. The visa cost 700 rupees, which was cheaper than I thought they would be but, unfortunately, we would have to return to pick them up. On the return journey the hapless rickshaw man suffered some kind of brake failure. Not a very smooth journey in either direction.

That evening, as it was Shane's birthday we were all meeting up at the *Kathmandu Guest House.* I wasn't able to find a card for him but I did see a copy of *The Little Prince* by Antoine de Saint Exupery and so bought that for him. I was happy to see Christian and Nepalese Tara there as well as almost everyone I had met on the trek. There were about twenty of us altogether, who then went round to *The Jazz Club.* It made me to smile to think about being on my own in Pokhara and thinking I needed to find a group to join before setting off on the trek.

While we were all together (American) Tara had suggested a trip to Bhaktapur the following day. In the end there were four of us who made the journey: Christian, the two Taras and myself. We travelled by public bus which was a bit of a squash as it was very crowded.

Bhaktapur was amazing with old temples and fascinating buildings. But the most interesting of all were the people, especially the children: there were hordes of them, playing, laughing and generally following us around. It was like stepping back in time into a medieval village. They were grinding corn and winnowing with big baskets used to sieve and sift the corn. We walked through a whole pathway of corn spread out like a golden carpet beneath our feet. Two young women were fashioning clay pots, pressing the clay into moulds.

I suppose we did stand out from the usual crowd, especially Tara, with her braided hair, colourful clothes and camera slung around her neck. She might have been The Pied Piper of Hamlin as a constant cluster of young children followed behind her as we walked together through the streets.

At one point, I was walking ahead with Christian discussing something deep if I recall. All of a sudden, we realised that the two Taras were no longer behind us. We walked back to the square and waited for about fifteen minutes. There was still no sign of them and so we made our way towards the main gate. The problem was that the gate we had made for was not the main gate.

Although we did eventually locate it, and waited for another twenty minutes in the square, there was still no sign of them. We decided to walk to the bus stop, where we eventually gave up, got on the bus and travelled back to Kathmandu without them. We discussed it and could think of nothing else to do. As a consolation, when we arrived in Kathmandu, the sky was the most beautiful colour: a brilliant gold and blue grey.

Later, just as I came out of the bathroom they arrived back. They too had spent some time looking for us and Tara (she) was not too pleased. She then suggested maybe going to Pashupatinath the following day. She told me she was meeting Sheldon at eight o'clock that evening to look at the photographs he had taken of them.

In direct contrast to my earlier reluctance to join her at the *Pleasure Home*, I sort of invited myself along, although I sensed she may not have wanted me there. Perhaps I had become more self-assured in the short time I had been with them all, but I ignored my intuition and went anyway. Christian and Axel joined us. We went to *The Roadhouse* whilst Tara (she) took Tara (he) to her room to give him her boots.

Sheldon arrived and, as they looked through the photos, it became clear Tara (she) was not happy at all. She shot off. Sheldon informed us that the cause of her unhappiness were his photographs. We all went to try to find her, but by the time Axel arrived it was 9.20pm and I was hungry. I said I was going to eat and Christian agreed we should go. We went to the *Shalimar* but the rest of the evening was a little strained, even though Sheldon and Christian handled everything sensitively and patiently.

I saw Christian at breakfast and said I may not go to Pashupatinath as I really did not want more of the same undercurrent of bad feeling. However, I told him my one regret was that I may not see Tara (he) to say goodbye. He suggested just going for a couple of hours but then Tara (she) arrived. She appeared to have recovered from her mood of the previous evening and so we set off to hire bikes.

The ride there was mainly through countryside instead of on the main roads and was much more enjoyable. Tara (he) was to meet us there. We eventually found him and he looked cool and smart as usual. We walked around, listened to a painted-faced old guy playing the flute. Then we saw the Milk Baba. He was supposed only ever to have drunk milk and not water. Aged forty-five, his hair comprised two and a half metres of Rasta plaits wound around his head. He did look in good nick. He told Christian he had travelled quite a lot in Italy and, as if to prove it, he brought out some photographs of himself taken there. He had not yet been to England or America. While we were there he actually performed a wedding ceremony and then Tara (he) asked the photographer, whom he knew, to take a photograph of our small group.

Our next stop was to watch the snake charmers, who were working with a python and two or three cobras. It was fascinating to see how they responded to the movement and music of *the pungi,* a flute-like instrument made from a gourd.

Tara led us on then towards the Bagmati river where we sat for a while watching the activity on the opposite bank. It appeared that two bodies had been laid to rest very near to the ghats where they would soon be burned. On our side of the river, there were a line of stalls nearby, no doubt for tourists like ourselves, including a Thangka stall run by another friend of Taras. By now the temperature had risen and to quench our thirst we each, rather incongruously in those surroundings, sat and drank a coke.

After a little while of sitting and chatting we made our way back to where we had parked our bikes. Tara (she) walked ahead with Christian and I walked behind with Tara (he). It was so peaceful and calm. I told him I would be leaving the day after tomorrow and may not see him again. He said he would come to the airport to see me off. I was surprised and touched by his comment. He asked me to write to him when I returned to England and I said of course I would.

On the way home, I was relying on Tara's (she) sense of direction through the lanes and unfortunately, we lost Christian. Tara let it be known she was sick of searching for people. I just kept on pedalling.

I had arranged to meet up with Janet, a woman from Bristol, that evening and I set off to meet her at 7.30pm at her hotel. I took the opportunity of ringing Julie from there. We managed just three minutes, which cost 425 rupees. She attempted to call me back but the hotel owner's wife had written down the wrong number and so she was unable to get through. I told her I would fax her from Bangkok.

Janet and I met up with Steve and Corinna, friends of hers, at a pizzeria, *Fire and Ice.* It was a pleasant change but rather expensive and so the whole evening proved to be rather draining financially. Steve, a gay American, from Cape Cod told me he lived in Bangkok and would be happy to show me a few places there as he too was flying out there on 24th but with RNAC. After dinner he showed us all some photographs he had taken in recent days. I was flicking through the second album and to my amazement there was one of Tara (he), clearly posing at the bottom of the restaurant steps. I realised he had probably taken it in Bhaktapur a couple of days before, when Tara had gone downstairs in the restaurant. I suspected Tara might have been gay as he was so beautiful as well as gentle. Certainly, he appealed to Steve. I asked would it be possible to get a copy of the photograph and we all arranged to meet up for breakfast the following day.

It made me realise how, as far as the backpacking community goes, it really was a small world. It occurred to me I had only one more day in Kathmandu. I had loved Nepal and its people and, apart from Tara's mini outburst, especially the last couple of days with her, Christian and Tara (he) would always be so memorable.

I was down for breakfast by 8.30am. Corinna arrived at nine and informed me she too was going to Bangkok. Janet came a little later and then finally Steve arrived. Steve said he would meet me at 7.30pm at the *Third Eye* to give me Tara's photograph.

I spent the rest of the day doing very little. First, I walked down to the Post Office with Karin's letter. I looked through Post Restante in vain. Clearly, no-one intended to write to me. I felt suitably ignored and disappointed. I wandered into a small gemstone shop and bought a silver ring. I was about to leave when I spotted a silver cobra with tiny stones for eyes. I immediately thought of Tara. It would be perfect for a present for him. I managed to haggle and get the price reduced to 750 rupees, which in current day value would be equivalent to about $7. I had only 100 rupees which I gave the shopkeeper as a deposit, because I knew the bank would be closed by the time I got there.

When I arrived back at the hotel, Kim had pushed a note through the door to say they were all meeting at the *New Orleans Jazz Bar* at 7.00pm. I went to meet Steve but he told me he had lost the photograph. Ah well. It was a particularly good one but I had my own from that day. They would do. I went on to the *New Orleans Jazz Bar* where I was happy to see Kim, Kathy, Tara (she) Axel and Paul. I could not believe that after my experience of chasing after a photo earlier in the evening I had forgotten to take my own camera.

It was very late when I got off to sleep because of the general noise and techno music blaring out from the Israelis on the roof. I had already packed most of my stuff but, even so, was awake very early, no doubt primed for the off. I went down for breakfast at 8.30am. On to the bank to draw out some cash and on the way back bumped into Tara, Kim and Wilco walking down to *Bluebells* for some breakfast. I said I'd catch up with them soon for a photo shoot. Then I went back to pick up my cobra before joining them all. Everyone was there and so I was able to take my group photo after all.

Back at the *Sagarmartha* I went to pay my bill. They informed me that Karin, who I had been sharing with, had not paid and so they expected me to pay the whole amount. I refused and eventually got off about 11.00am, not before I had bumped into Janet, who had brought the photograph from Steve. I was so pleased to have it and then felt guilty for having doubted Jeff. I immediately went round to thank him and got his number for when he arrives in Bangkok.

I took a taxi to the airport and arrived about 11.15am. To my delight I had only just stepped out of the taxi, when I heard my name being called. It was Tara. I really couldn't believe he had remembered. I was so thrilled and took great pleasure in giving him the cobra. I think he liked it. He looked delighted. He asked me had I slept well, perhaps because when I met him for the second time, I recall telling him I had not slept well. When he asked me why, I said it was usually because I was thinking too much. I was amazed again that he had remembered. He said he would look into English teaching in Nepal for me. Then he produced a long cream coloured scarf in a delicate chiffon material and placed it round my neck, a wonderful Nepalese custom when people are leaving to go on a journey. I said goodbye, left him and went for a coffee in the air-conditioned restaurant. I could not stop smiling.

I was sad to be leaving Nepal but knew I would always possess warm, cherished memories of friendships, however fleeting, made in Pokhara and on the trek. Soon I would be winging my way towards Bangkok, a city I had assumed to be completely off limits only a couple of months earlier.

Thailand: yet another country. What new experiences awaited me there?

THAILAND

BANGKOK

Flight TG312 was twenty-five minutes late taking off but, after the usual 'heart slightly in the mouth' take off, everything went well. The meal of seafood and rice was delicious and we touched down in Bangkok at 6.15pm as they were one hour fifteen minutes ahead of Nepalese time. It was just beginning to get dark.

I discovered that Bangkok airport was ultra-modern. There was no delay in picking up my pack and then heading straight outside to get a standard fare taxi to the *New Siam Guest House.* I knew it was very near to Khao San Road but the taxi driver told me he would just drop me in Khao San Road as he didn't know exactly where the guest house was. I wasn't too happy about that. I didn't know how long the road was and therefore how far I would need to walk with my pack to find the *New Siam.* In truth, there was still a little apprehension about another new place, especially from the picture I had in my imagination about Bangkok.

He was a taxi driver after all and so why didn't he know? Maybe the peaceful vibe of Nepal was still with me as I chose to say nothing, or maybe I was very much aware of being, for the moment, in his hands in this foreign city. After a very short time I engaged him in conversation, asking about a garland he bought from a young man at a traffic stop. He told me it was Buddhist. I then told him I believed in much of the Buddhist philosophy, which was indeed true. This opened up the conversation more and he asked why I was on my own, with no husband or family. Why did I want to go to Khao San Road? It wasn't a good place for someone (read 'woman'), on their own. Then he asked me if I liked football and confessed his favourite team was Manchester United. He was thrilled when I told him I came from Manchester. From that moment on we were buddies.

He took me straight to the *New Siam* which was just around the corner at the very end of Khao San Road. By the time we arrived it was 10.25pm and, from the moment I walked inside, I liked the look of the place. Best of all, there was a brightly lit restaurant/café on the ground floor, with one side open to the small side street. This was a huge advantage to me as it meant I would not have to go out in the evening in search of somewhere to eat. (I intended to 'suss out' this small area of Bangkok at my own steady pace). I could sit in the comfortable restaurant reading until as late as I might wish. That suited me fine.

It was not the cheapest at 160 baht, which I calculated was around £4.30, as opposed to the places I had stayed in Nepal, where a room was usually under £2. Here, I would be paying for a single room, with a shower outside, off the corridor. However, it was clean and the hotel itself very near to the river. I was only going to be there for a week. According to my calculations, it would allow me another 180 baht (£4 to £5) per day for food and whatever else I may need and still allow me to stay well within my budget. I faxed Julie to let her know I had arrived safely for more than *one night in Bangkok*!

The room was basic, the bed uncomfortable and the mattress lumpy. Despite all this, I managed to sleep. After breakfast I set out to explore and headed for Khao San Road. I needed to replenish my meagre 'wardrobe' and so bought a couple of tee shirts, two pairs of shorts and a sarong. I ventured on to the broad Chao Phraya River from Phra Athit pier, which I discovered was only a short distance from the *New Siam*. The boat was not very big but, as I thought, it was much cooler on the water. I happened to sit next to a couple who were heading for the markets in Chinatown. As my river journey was impromptu, not having planned anything for such a short stay in Bangkok, I decided I would disembark when they did. I was not overly impressed with the markets, perhaps because I had never been a great shopper, but I imagined that Chinatown would be a great place to visit in the evening.

Back at the hotel, I requested a change of room, making sure I tested the bed before making the exchange. It was much more comfortable. I had a tentative plan to meet Tara in Koh Tao in time for her birthday on 10th June and so decided I would travel first to Ko Samui, as I had been informed that the monsoon rains would begin towards the end of June. Although not on my 'to do' list, I was mysteriously drawn into a women's hairdressers just across from the New Siam. 'Cut it as short as possible', I told them. When I next stepped out into the street, I sported a haircut shorter than any I had ever worn before, apart from maybe at twelve months of age.

It felt great, quite daring somehow. Is it just me, or do many women change their hairstyle at moments of change or crisis, or when they are feeling down. I was feeling pretty low. Everyone seemed to be with someone else. Ah, the curse of being alone. Not something I was totally unfamiliar with at

114

certain times during my life, but just occasionally it was harder to bear.

I took another trip on the river, this time to the GPO as I had promised to send off a registered letter for Emily. Back at base, I wandered into Khao San Road to browse and, as if my wishes had magically come true, heard someone shout my name. It was Paul from the trek, who was sitting outside a bar. I joined him in a beer and a much-missed good natter before going across the street to get something to eat. To my surprise, yet another person I knew— Janet's Swedish friend, Corinna, was there and so we joined her. I enjoyed a delicious vegetarian Thai curry. I was beginning to find my 'inner' balance once more.

Paul suggested meeting for breakfast the following day and then going to Chinatown and so I decided to change my booking to Ko Samui to Tuesday 28th. It would also give me another day to send off my parcel containing some of the things I no longer needed, as well as those I wanted to keep safe. When I returned to the New Siam, as if I had earned a bonus in the connection department, I learnt I had received a fax from Julie.

I slept well, but woke with a bit of a headache, no doubt due to the beers I had quaffed the previous day. When I eventually met up with Paul he told me he had decided to go to Koh Tao and then possibly on to work in Korea. He was setting off at 1.00pm and so that left me the afternoon to go back to the Post Office and send off my parcel, which I was told would probably take about two months before it arrived. I then went to pick up my sleep sheet (fashioned like a sleeping bag) and discovered that it wasn't silk, as I had thought when I ordered it. The tailor told me it was 80% silk and 20% cotton, 'Better for machine washing,' he told me. I later found out from another tailor it was probably polyester. Another lesson for the learning as I should have refused to pay for it, except I was pushed for time and I conceded it would be much lighter than my old, and now very worn, cotton one with which I had started out.

For someone who is not a natural shopper, Koh San Road seemed to draw me in. Tuesday morning saw me there on a last 'mad' shopping spree. I bought a small Walkman/radio, a few bootleg tapes, a pair of Thai pants, another sleeveless top and a cap. I then dashed back to the New Siam to pack before sharing a tuk-tuk to the station with a Parisian couple. The driver sped through the streets like a lunatic, *zut alors*, but at least he got us there. The sleeper train was comfortable and, although I remained seated during the journey, it was the cheapest way to travel and I did sleep most of the way. We arrived in Surat Thani twelve hours later at 6.30am. With half an hour to spare, I had chance to grab a coffee and a croissant and then it was straight on to the bus which took us to the ferry port.

It was already hot when we set sail for Ko Samui at 8.00am. The boat was crowded and I found myself sitting at the front nicely exposed to the rays of the early morning sun. Another omission in the planning was not realising how hot it would be despite the early hour. Well, I was paying for it now, as my face slowly began to turn a pale shade of crimson. I had been looking forward to relaxing in the sun on this beautiful island but this was not a good start.

KO SAMUI

Once we arrived at Na-Thon pier I took a tuk-tuk to Lamai beach. As the morning wore on, despite having applied the sunscreen, I began to feel faint. I was trudging along in my search for somewhere to stay. My pack was becoming heavier by the minute. I decided to abandon my search and stopped at the nearest place. It was a relief to rest for a while and get something to drink but the place appeared deserted; not the ambience I was looking for at all.

I left my pack in the room and wandered not very far up the road, only to discover *Utopia* – a wonderfully apposite name. There was a covered restaurant with an open terrace overlooking the beach. The room I was shown looked very clean, despite the primitive shower and a crack in a couple of the windows. I told them I would like to move in there tomorrow and even managed to negotiate a 10% reduction. That evening, I returned to eat in their restaurant and enjoyed a delicious Thai vegetable curry. The film showing on the small T.V. screen was Maeve Binchy's *Circle of Friends* and I noticed in the credits that Andrew Davies, who had been my workshop tutor on Skyros the previous year, had written the screen adaptation. What a coincidence.

The following day I woke feeling a little down and my period, which was rather late, finally arrived. I decided before moving to *Utopia* to check out another place I had heard of – *Coral Cove Resort* – probably with the intention of hiding away again. When eventually I managed to locate the place, it seemed O.K. but somehow didn't feel right. I have learned, as I've got older, always to trust my intuition. So, *Utopia* it was. When I arrived back there, I must have been riding an unusual wave of assertiveness as I asked whether I could see another room, which I had heard would be vacated the following day.

Later that day Scott and his girlfriend Karen, who I'd met only briefly, started chatting to me. They were leaving *Utopia* and bought drinks for everyone they had met there. There was Wolf, a Thai and Karl, who was English, as well as Richard and Star, a young American couple and their little boy Jesse. I sampled some Sang Thip Thai whiskey, which I later learned is actually not whiskey but rum and best drunk with coke. It's known in Thailand as Sang Thip Royal Thai liquor. Having been alcohol free in India and Nepal, and tending never to drink during the day, I didn't take very much at all. I realised though, just as I had after the trek, how much I was enjoying being with this group of friendly people.

Amongst the group were a couple of English girls, Beatrice

and Philippa, who had just arrived from Indonesia, where I was heading. They shared quite a few stories of their time there, Philippa waxing lyrical about the beautiful bodies of young Indonesian men. This cross fertilisation of experiences between travellers I still found fascinating. It provided a link, sometimes a bond, between comparative strangers and helped in preparing them for what they might expect as they moved on to another country!

Utopia was clearly a popular meeting place for travellers, no doubt because of its central position, the bar and also the restaurant. However, Philippa told me they were not staying at *Utopia*, but at a place known as *The Hut* and only paying 30 baht each. I felt quite guilty and uneconomical as I was paying 135 baht (equivalent then to about £4.50 per day), which I was aware was double what I had paid in Nepal.

The following morning, I awoke with an attack of the blues, even telling myself that maybe I should just go home. What was going on? Surely it could not be down to guilt about my slightly expanded budget. I knew I was simultaneously escaping aspects of my life and searching for something, maybe someone, maybe simply my Self, whoever she was. Such a mission was bound to create highs and lows.

I saw Jim, the (female) owner of *Utopia* at breakfast and

she said she had a couple more rooms to show me just next door to the one I was in. The one I chose seemed palatial compared to mine. It was light and spacious, with no gaps in the floorboards and all the windows fitted well. There was a separate shower cubicle in the bathroom and a flushing loo. Never mind Utopia, I thought I had arrived in heaven. And then a shadowy thought crept in: *if only there was someone to share some of it with.* I took a deep breath and successfully shoved the depressing thought to the back of my mind.

Heaven and *Utopia*: what a combination! There was not to be even a smidgeon of room for regrets. And speaking of rooms, the number of the one I eventually settled on was 101 which, in Aldous Huxley's *Brave New World,* was the basement torture chamber in *The Ministry of Love.* What wonderful irony! My intuition had been spot-on as I was clearly meant to be here at *Utopia.* But as part of my 'search' would I be subjected to my worst nightmare, fear or phobia? Maybe? I had yet to find out. But, given the odds, I reckoned it was a risk worth taking.

At 2.15pm I ventured on to the beach for the first time. It was beautiful, the perfect setting in which to chill out. But after an hour the extreme heat drove me inside for a cool drink on the terrace. I went out again at 4.00pm and stayed for a couple of hours. As the sun began to sink towards the horizon it was so picturesque: just below the terrace, huge palm trees fringing the beach appeared to bow in homage to the Gulf of Thailand and beyond, the South China Sea stretching as far as the eye could see. I knew I had found 'my place' here at *Utopia*. It was everything I had hoped it would be. I read for a while and then went back to my bungalow to shower and change.

Back in the restaurant by 7.00pm there was no-one else around and so Rush, who normally served behind the bar, came to chat to me. He had been part of the group of people I met when I first called into *Utopia* and on that occasion told everyone he was 28, as that day just happened to be his birthday. In the short space of ten minutes he had asked why I was alone, where was my family, how old were my children and then, quite unselfconsciously, how old was I. When I told him he noticeably gulped and made some remark about his mother being a similar age. Ah well, what could I say.

But then quite openly he told me I looked young – my face, my body and the way I walked. He went on to say, with a big grin on his face, that in Thailand women of 48 walked around bent double and then he proceeded to hobble across the floor by way of demonstration. Whether his compliments contained only a grain of truth was not the issue. I was not used to such openness. It was refreshing.

Anyhow, by then, more people began to appear. There was Richie, Star and little Jesse, then Philippa and Theresa appeared and then Wolf and one or two others I had not met before. We all then sat and watched a video starring Johnny Depp, which I enjoyed. Then I went with Richie and Star to the supermarket and paid half towards some Sang Thip and coke.

When we returned, the others had carried some of the tables from the restaurant down on to the beach for us all to celebrate our own 'full moon' party. There were about twenty people around the table and a wonderful time was had by all. I got a little drunk and smoked my second cigarette of the trip. Much later on, I took a short stroll along the beach with Wolf, who told me how he had met his Canadian girlfriend here at Lamai beach. He explained that the 'art feature', involving lighted candles, which he had constructed earlier on the beach in front of *Utopia,* was in her honour.

By 3.00am everyone had disappeared. I was alone out there on the, now deserted, beach, with a silver-white full moon suspended just above the far horizon. It was magical. I did not want to go inside and so I went back to my room to get the Walkman I bought in Bangkok. I played the Van Morrison tape and danced to the track, 'Moondance.' How fitting I thought. Memories flooded back of similar scenes that had touched me.

In a little over eleven weeks I would be 49. Since arriving on this island, surrounded by mostly young people, I seemed to be morphing into an impressionable teenager? Did it matter? And then my eye followed the silver pathway over the black sea towards the moon. That must be it. I was moonstruck.

The following day, feeling more than a little introspective, I decided it would not be good to spend time alone. Along with Andrea and Janine, two Canadian girls as well as Wolf, we hired a jeep to explore the island. We stopped first at one end of Chaweng beach. It was even more beautiful than Lamai. The sand was much whiter and the turquoise sea much shallower for quite a way out and very, very hot. I took a turn at driving the small jeep, which wasn't easy as the road was very narrow. Our final destination was 'Grandfather Rocks'; a phallic arrangement of large rocks perched on top of a headland. Wolf took great pleasure in posing for a photograph in exactly the right place in front of them.

On the Sunday, I decided I would have a quiet day. It was 11.00am before I got down on to the beach and, as it was so hot, I spent quite a bit of time swimming. I needed the exercise as I had been lazing around far too much. Late afternoon, as the temperature cooled, I walked into Lamai thinking I might try to find somewhere else to eat that evening. I bought a sarong as well as some much-needed sun block, some soap and postcards. However, there was nowhere I fancied to eat and so that evening found me once more in the restaurant at Utopia.

At 8.00pm the usual crowd arrived and we ended up down on the beach once more. I was introduced to a mad game involving crossing hands and tapping once or twice, the loser having to down shots of Sang Thip. Unfortunately, I lost quite a few times and so, once again, drank more than I intended. Soon, Philippa and I called a halt and together went to Bauhaus, a bar with a dancefloor, a few minutes' walk away. Later on, Leo, Karl, Wolf, Rush and MK all turned up. We danced for a couple of hours, leaving about 4.00am. Another very late night (or early morning) but I really enjoyed myself. Philippa is the same age as Julie and with a similar bubbly personality.

The following day, not surprisingly, I was tired. I spent most of the morning sitting chatting to Andreas (the Austrian) and Wolf, intermittently, while attempting to write postcards and a letter to a friend back home, which I then went off to post. On them I mentioned Poste Restante in the hope that, by the time I arrived in Sydney, I may have received some mail. At 4.30pm I went for a swim, a hundred strokes along the shore line and back again. I intended to do the same each day, maybe twice a day.

All my life I had been active, playing team sports up to the age of 32. I played hockey in the winter and tennis in the summer and only stopped at the point where I had started studying full-time for a degree after my divorce. I was studying Literature, History and Philosophy and so there was a lot of required reading. This last, combined with looking after my two young children, I believed would leave me no time for sport. It turned out to be a mistake; too drastic a reversal for my body to take. It was used to moving and now it was being forced to sit as `I read for long periods. Not surprisingly, when the three years were up and frustratingly, just as I was setting off for a much-needed break in France, my back decided to give up. I wasn't about to make that mistake again.

I had intended once again looking for somewhere else to eat, but a slight stomach upset (probably as a result of imbibing too much Sang Thip) meant it would be more sensible to stay closer to 'home'. As I sat in the restaurant, MK, a colleague of Rush's and a really pleasant guy, came over to sit with me for about half an hour. He told me he was

31. Although he had danced with me for a while at *Bauhaus*, I knew he was quite shy. He told me he had two jobs, this one at *Utopia* and another one as night auditor at a big hotel. He worked sixteen hours a day. MK, Rush and Ang, a lovely young girl I had come to know there, all worked long hours. As MK revealed a little of his life to me, I pondered on how people such as they, working in these tourist places truly felt about travellers, who have the time and resources to come and relax, albeit on a temporary basis, in their part of the world.

Saturday 8th June and unusually, I woke to a bleak, gloomy day. In the night, there had been a storm and it continued as a deluge of a downpour until about 4.00pm. For most of the day, I sat in the restaurant, chatting occasionally, writing up my journal and reading my book. It was really lovely to watch the curtain of rain against the bright green of the garden. It looked so lush and smelled really fresh.

I had met Lucy, a German speaking Swiss girl the day before. She was travelling with her sister and a friend, who unfortunately had been taken into hospital with a serious pain. As the rain poured down we sat chatting in the shelter of the restaurant. She told me she enjoyed talking to me, which was lovely to hear, given I must be a similar age to her mother. Perhaps that was why. She gave me a list of places to stay in Malaysia and Indonesia.

At 6.00pm, after a walk along the beach I returned to the restaurant, where M.K. made me a 'special' coffee, possibly containing a liqueur. I took it on to the beach to drink while I read my book. It was very good. Later, after a shower and change I actually went out to eat, but was thwarted as the storm had left behind a huge lake and the road was completely submerged. Another restaurant nearby was dead and so I returned to Utopia. I sat with Ian a Kiwi and a Scottish couple, Carey and George from Thurso in the very far north of Scotland, not far from John O'Groats. Amazingly, I was able to tell them I had been there when I was sixteen, to visit my aunt and an uncle who had worked at Dounreay Atomic Power Station. What a small world! I ordered one beer and then went on water for the rest of the evening.

UNSETTLED AFTER THE STORMS

During the night there were more storms, which continued until late morning. Ian had told me about a road that circled into Lamai beach along the back way and so I set off to explore. It took me about an hour, with a stop for some lunch at *Will Wait* restaurant, but then it began to get uncomfortably hot and sticky as I walked. The last stretch of my walk was more pleasant along the beach, as the road was still flooded.

In the afternoon, I began to sense a restless energy stirring within me and could find nothing of interest to say or do. At 5.00pm I decided to go for a swim in an attempt to curb it. Maybe it was the change in the weather. Despite welcoming the cooler air after recent rains, I knew the storms had somehow affected my mood. I had become so used to days filled to the brim with sunshine.

The following day the sun returned and, after lunch, I met up with Marie-Therese again, an Austrian woman travelling with her young son. Yesterday she had been suffering from a bad cold. Anyhow, feeling better today, she had booked a massage on the beach for later on and asked did I want to join her. I agreed, although when it came to it I felt rather self-conscious, even though the beach was not too crowded and we were tucked away under a palm tree. At home I had always enjoyed having a massage. There had only been one occasion when I definitely did not. The masseuse in question may only have been in training, or new to the practice, but her anxiety was transmitted to me through her reluctance to touch. Still, Thai massage was renowned for being different and this one I enjoyed very much. Afterwards, Marie-Therese sat and chatted with me over coffee and then later she joined me for dinner.

I was just about to turn in at 11.30pm when Tom, Ute and Rush asked if I wanted to go to Chaweng to the *Green Mango*. So there I was, perched on the back of Rush's motor bike zooming along the narrow roads of Ko Samui as midnight approached. Surely, this was some strange time warp I found myself in: a Dorian Grey experience, definitely a delayed adolescence. I trusted Rush, I knew Tom and Ute and we were going to a new place to dance. What more could I have wished for? The *Green Mango* appealed to me, with more variety than the Bauhaus. As Rush was working the following day, we left 'early' at 3.00am. He dropped me off forty-five minutes later at Utopia and, despite the hour, I could not resist sitting on the beach for five minutes before turning in.

The following day the rain had cleared, although it had left in its wake a sea that was far too choppy to entice me in for a swim. Still introspective, I was not in the mood for chatting or even for reading. After lunch, the sun appeared long enough for me to bask in its rays for an hour. In my pensive mood I only wanted music and so, as the sun went in, I listened to Van Morrison, then Youssou N'Dour. It was relaxing, sitting in the shade with a cool breeze blowing off the ocean, doing nothing but listening to music.

But by the evening, my mood was low, eventually choosing to sit on my own to eat in the restaurant. I was feeling so disconnected I had to take myself off, away from everyone. I sat on my little balcony outside my bungalow and wrote out how I was feeling. Later, Rush came along and sat with me for a while. It was very sweet of him. I went into the bar later and, between customers, we talked some more. He spoke frankly about certain aspects of his life which, unsurprisingly, as with the rest of us, was more complicated than his image projected.

I awoke the following day with thoughts of when I should be going home: *Freudian slip* … moving on. In any case I no longer had a home, or at least a house. In setting off on this trip, I realised I had set myself free for the very first time in my life and maybe I was experiencing a feeling of disorientation, of loss, unable quite to find my bearings. I was aware I had definitely fallen into the trap of feeling 'at home' here at *Utopia*. I had allowed myself to become close to certain people: one or two who had been travelling through yes, but mainly those who worked here, those who I saw day in, day out: MK, Ang and especially Rush.

It is so easy when you are on your own for any length of time to crave closeness. At least that is my experience. It's where to draw the line— those boundaries again. Was this the very first time I had found myself in amongst people, but essentially alone, with no close ties of my own? This effect was compounded even more, as it was so physically difficult to maintain regular contact with people back home. Added to which, I had spent nearly two weeks now with so much time to spare and no agenda; something I would never experience in the normal course of events.

I had chosen to take this time out of my usual existence and, in so doing, had literally cut myself off. It was as if I had entered a parallel universe; one whose parameters I had yet to discover. Sitting around in the restaurant, at times during the day and most evenings as well, meant I had more chance to observe what was going one, to watch people as they went about their business. Maybe I was simply projecting on to this world and these gentle people, my own inner sense of confusion, as I searched for a place to belong.

The truth was I enjoyed their company and so the following evening, their two motorbikes heading for Chewang and a cool breeze blowing through my hair, Rush, MK, Noi and me found ourselves once again at the *Green Mango*. It was my kind of dance music when we arrived. Unfortunately, it soon changed to techno, which I can't stand. The four of us sat at a table on a raised floor. It was in a dark corner and, at one point, as I got up to dance, walking down the steps, I missed my footing and fell. I could see how it might look like a drunken fall, but it happened soon after we arrived. The bottom step was not lit like the others but seemed to merge into the floor. Still, I felt stupid and I was painfully aware of how it might have been embarrassing for them, especially MK.

We moved on to the *Reggae Pub,* a much smaller place. Noi and Rush bought some food, some kind of spicy meat, which I really enjoyed. I never imagined that on this trip I might also regress, turning once more into a smoker and a carnivore. I had stopped smoking twenty years before. True, I had dabbled on the trek, but Ko Samui had been my undoing. Yet another 'adolescent' trait I would have to knock on the head before long. What was happening to me?

The following day I showered and, very tired and slightly hungover, I stumbled into breakfast about 9.30am. Noi was busy working in the garden and MK looked as fresh as a daisy. There was no sign of Rush. Ian had a copy of Sunday's paper, which he let me read over breakfast. I was shocked to read of a bombing in Manchester the previous day. The Provisional IRA (Irish Republican Army) had detonated a powerful 1,500-kilogram truck bomb on Corporation Street in the centre of Manchester. I felt sick as I read it. Saturday was the day my friend might possibly be shopping in town. Paul and Steph occasionally would drive into Manchester to shop.

I sat on the beach with Ian for a while and then decided to send a fax to Paul, asking him to fax me back. It was cloudy but still hot and so I stayed on the beach for most of the day, feeling restless and anxious. I was aware of really missing family and friends back home. I went in at 4.30pm, had a shower and then lay down under the ceiling fan to get cool. The next thing I knew there was a loud knocking at my door. It was MK, asking if I was O.K. I had fallen asleep and now it was 8.00pm and he told me everyone was wondering where I was as I had not shown up at my 'usual' time for dinner. Such lovely, caring and considerate people, I was so touched. I was aware of feeling very sad; missing everyone at home and sad too that I would be leaving here soon—another separation: a scenario I was not at all unfamiliar with.

Later, not feeling very hungry I sat at the bar with Ian and ate a salad and some garlic bread. He told me that earlier when I hadn't shown, everyone had been worried about me. Rush asked me if I was sad, maybe homesick? I said I was, a little and sad too about leaving Utopia and all the friends I had made. He asked how long I would be staying. I told him another few days. He looked genuinely disappointed and suggested I wait until Sunday when MK would be back then we could have a leaving 'do'. I was unsure about waiting almost another week. By then I would have been in Thailand for a month. I did have a two-month visa. I decided to wait to see how I felt in the next couple of days.

When I went into breakfast the following day I was delighted to have received a three-page fax from Steph, filling me in with all the gossip from home. It made my day. I decided to go into Nathon to get some information about train and bus times for when I do decide to leave. It looked as if a bus to Hat Yai might be the best bet, then possibly on to Penang from there. I was also on the search for another bikini but had no luck at all. Wandering around in the heat of the day by then was draining. I just wanted to get on to the beach and go for a swim. I had bought a second-hand copy of D.H.

Lawrence's *Women in Love* and a passage on the first page entitled *The Beginning* caught my eye and spoke to me:

> 'She reached up, like Eve reaching to the apples on the tree of knowledge, and she kissed him, though her passion was a transcendent fear of the thing he was, touching his face with her infinitely delicate, encroaching, wondering fingers. Her fingers went over the mould of his face, over his features. How perfect and foreign he was – ah, how dangerous! ... this was the glistening forbidden apple.'

After dinner and the film (which I gave up on), I watched football in *Utopia* with Rush. We shared the remainder of my Sang Thip. I told him I was going to the Bauhaus to watch England v Holland, so he told me he would come with me. 'How could I go on my own? I would need someone to take care of me.' This last said jokingly. By the time it got to midnight, he looked so tired I didn't think he would want to go, but he said he did.

There had been another heavy storm during the evening. It was still raining a little and very wet on the ground. We walked two doors away to the *Pavilion Resort* to get MK's motor bike. He was so busy however, he could not get away and so we ended up walking. It was 1.00am by the time we arrived at the Bauhaus and my clothes felt rather damp, but at least it was cool. Rush suggested a dance. I danced and he watched and then we went across the road and sat at a stall eating a hamburger. It was delicious. He then led me next door to his friend's place, which was partly open to the street, and so I ended up watching the match with him and about a dozen of his friends. They seemed happy to accept this 'somewhat older' ferang woman as one of his mates. It was all very natural. When the match had finished Rush arranged for one of his friends to give me a lift back to Utopia in his jeep. The whole evening had been another memorable experience.

CLOSE CONNECTIONS

Not surprisingly, I was late waking up the following day. It was almost lunch time when I ate breakfast. Ian, sitting at the next table to me, asked about the match. At the next table were Rob and Caroline from New Zealand. Earlier in the week Caroline very kindly had offered me a room at their place when I eventually arrived in New Zealand. They were sitting with an older couple, Brian and Patsy, who were English but had been living in Melbourne for 34 years. I wrote another fax to Steph and then went on the beach. It had been very dull but, by then, the sun had come through. As it disappeared behind the clouds, I went for a couple of good long swims. In between, I read more of my book. I love D.H. Lawrence and so the afternoon flew by.

By about 6.15pm I was showered and sitting at the bar in the restaurant. Rush and MK were very busy and so I went to sit at my favourite spot on the terrace overlooking the beach. The Australian couple were in the sea very close together. I felt a pang of envy. I did so want to feel close to someone.

Just then, Rush came and sat below me on the steps and

asked what I was doing.

I replied, 'Watching – just like you'.

He responded by saying, 'Watching, thinking?'

I smiled and said, 'Now I can watch you, as you are here in front of me.'

'You always have me in your eye,' he said. I loved the image and thought later, I would write it in a poem, maybe the following day.

He then began to open up to me about his memories of the past. How across the sea, in the direction he pointed, was the South China Sea and how, when he was about four or five years old, boatloads of refugees from Vietnam landed on this very beach in front of us. He told me he remembered seeing many men raping a woman and then throwing her body into the sea. Most of the refugees were shot right there on the beach.

He described the beach as it was then. There were no bungalows, only palm trees. No-one ventured out on to the beach at night as it was a dangerous place, not as it is now, where people walk along the beach and hold parties there. He went on to tell me that only people from Samui owned land in Lamai. So, the German who ran the rowdy bar next door, was only allowed to rent. In Chewang, though, there were some ferangs who owned land as they had so much money. Many of his friends too had made a lot of money from land rental and did not have to work as he did. He told me he would like to be a Communist, but then laughed at the thought of it. When he goes out he told me everywhere is the same: *Green Mango, Reggae Club* or *Bauhaus* — everyday, same-same.

He seemed in a really wistful, philosophical mood. I guessed he liked talking to me as I had the time to pay attention and to listen and because I understood everything when he spoke. I had noticed that a lot of other people did not understand a lot of his English. I also believed he knew, like me, that despite his unusual lifestyle, given more time we could perhaps have become close. Yet, how much easier was it to imagine such possibilities when they were unlikely to happen. How much more potent are one's feelings at merely the concept of 'forbidden fruit?'

At dinner I sat with Ian. Most of the films showing at *Utopia* did not appeal to me, but this was *Pulp Fiction*. It was very good and I do like John Travolta. Whilst sitting there, I was intent on not keeping Rush 'in my eye' during the evening and I noticed that he was aware of it. It was made easier as, sitting at the next table, was a couple I had not seen before. He was possibly Thai, but I couldn't be sure and she was European. He was very attractive: tall, with a beautiful face and head and reminded me of someone I once knew.

I realised that I would have to move on and mix with other people, get out of my own head. There had been too many moments when I seemed to be a seething, raging mass of hormones; more like an adolescent girl than a forty-eight-year-old woman.

I had not done any research and knew no-one in a similar position, but it occurred to me that maybe there was typically a final flurry of hormonal activity just before the menopause set in: a kind of 'raging against the dying of the light' to alter the context of the Dylan Thomas poem. That stage of my existence could not be too far off, lurking below the horizon, I reminded myself.

Around 11.00pm someone, possibly Rush's girlfriend, turned up with his motorbike. By about 11.20pm I decided to retire to my balcony to read. I was too wide awake to attempt sleep. No doubt having become used to such late nights or more accurately, early mornings. About twenty minutes later, Rush started up the bike but, just before leaving spotted me sitting there. As he passed he called out my name in that beautiful sing-song Thai way and added, 'Not sleeping?' I called out 'Goodnight', which he returned, before leaving. I put my book aside and wrote up my journal. I seemed to have more I wanted to get down on the page every day now and so I did not want to leave it too long.

The German restaurant next door was still 'swinging'. Pui and No Tail, Jim's two dogs, were asleep, one on the other chair and the other at my feet. Jim came by about 12.30am and told me she had managed to send my fax. I thanked her and hoped I might get one, or maybe more, back in the next few days.

Most of the following day was spent on the beach, with a break for lunch, during which Caroline taught me how to play backgammon. By the time I had showered and appeared in the restaurant for dinner, the sky had turned very black in parts. The view from the terrace was very beautiful and dramatic. I went back to get my camera and took a photograph of MK standing at the top of the steps. Rush was in a very jokey mood. Earlier on, he had called out to me to come into the restaurant, saying it was 'sad hour'. He proceeded to explain that if 'happy hour' was when drinks were half price, then 'sad hour' was when the price was doubled.

Ian came over to sit with me and together we watched the film 'Congo' which, I was not surprised to discover, was for me at least, a bit of a let-down. We chatted for about an hour afterwards. He had told Ang earlier that, just like Rush, he did not like families. He told me he had not got on with his father at all. He did not mention his mother, but he told me he had three sisters and gets on O.K. with them. How many lone travellers were there who felt more 'at home' out in the world than they ever did at home? It struck me then that I could relate to that.

The sea had been quite choppy most days. So much so, I had not wanted to swim for too long. I learnt how to swim aged five, but had always lacked complete confidence as a swimmer. I tried to compensate for not swimming by doing regular stretches each day, but it wasn't quite the same. Late afternoon, and there was another storm and at dinner the electricity went off again. The inclement weather seemed to me to reflect my moments of inner turmoil.

At dinner, I sat at a large table with the two New Zealand couples, an Australian couple and two Americans: all very pleasant people but, in the end, I found the level of noise generated by their conversation just too loud for me to take. I made my apologies early and moved to sit with Ian at the bar. It was then he told me that Rush would not be coming out with us on my supposed 'leaving do' the following night.

Sunday morning and at breakfast there was only Jim, Ang and Um in the restaurant. MK later told me Rush had gone to Surat Thani with a friend who was going to be a monk (surely said tongue-in-cheek I thought, although delivered with a serious expression). For my party that evening a group of us headed up to the *Bauhaus*. Ian never ventured out and so there were only two people I knew – MK and Noi. There was also Maun and Pye, who was Rush's girlfriend. I was in their hands.

We went first to a karaoke place where they showed scantily-clad, white skinned Thai girls on a big screen. Noi sang one or two Thai songs and then I had my big moment, when I sang *Desperado*, a Carpenters' song I like. Not having haunted any karaoke joints much before, I was not prepared for my rendition being played back. I cringed a little but it sounded OK. Then we went to the *Bauhaus,* where much 'non-stop' dancing was enjoyed by all. In the rare moments between the dance, we all quaffed Sang Thip, what else? And then Maun bought some tequila. But by 2.45am I had had enough although, not wanting to break up the party, I encouraged them to stay. I kissed MK on the cheek, said goodnight and set off to walk back on my own. On the way I called at the hamburger bar I had visited with Rush.

I was aware now of the time fast approaching when I would be leaving this place which had become my 'home' for the last few weeks. Moments of anxiety, almost panic overtook me although I knew that, once on the road again, they would subside. Something to do with leaving and separation, a pattern I had become familiar with in my life. I had vaguely planned to leave the following day on the Friday.

Rush, who had returned yesterday after his trip, chatted to me briefly and told me a little about where they had been, admitting once more how, afterwards, he realised it was 'all too much'. He had looked sad yesterday, even melancholic I thought, perhaps a reflection of this apparent weariness that seemed to consume him when he reflected on certain aspects of his life. I told him I would miss him after I left.

He laughed in response and said that if I came back to Thailand one day he and MK could show me other parts on the mainland. I knew that MK loved Kanchanaburi in the north, as he mentioned it once to me. He had told me about the Buddhist shrines nearby and the beautiful National Parks, where elephants roamed. What I did not know at the time was that in 1942, Kanchanaburi was under Japanese

148

control. It was here that Asian forced labourers and Allied POWs (Prisoners of War), building the infamous Burma Railway, constructed a bridge, an event immortalised in the films *The Bridge on the River Kwai.*

My very last day at Utopia and it was scorching hot. I was up quite early, had breakfast and was on the beach before 10.00am. An hour was all I could manage and so by 11.00am I went back and showered. I was sitting in the restaurant waiting for Jim when Rush appeared. Jim apparently had a few things to do and the place was quite empty. Rush came over and sat with me. We talked a little about his life; how he knew the drinking and smoking when he was out with friends were 'too much', a phrase he had used so often before. It seemed to me to express a certain level of awareness but at the same time his tone of voice reflected a kind of hopelessness to effect any change. Typically, he quickly switched to a more light-hearted topic and we talked about music and singing. He asked who sang 'In the Summertime' as he liked that song. I understood the appeal for him. At the time I could not recall who it was but later, remembered it was Mungo Jerry.

I left with Jim about 1.30pm and bought my ticket for the ferry and bus to Hat Yai. When I returned I went on the beach. On this *last* day I was calculating how many *last times* there were and this beautiful beach had been a big part of my stay at *Utopia*. Still, I could only manage an hour as I also wanted a 'last time' to sit in my favourite place on the porch of my bungalow and write my journal as I was cooling down. Rush soon appeared and sat below on his motor bike. He asked me if I'd got my ticket and how much it was. Was I sure it was the right one? Had Jim got it for me? Could he look at it? After all the questioning he seemed satisfied everything was O.K. And then he asked, exactly as Tara had, if I would write to him.

As a person he was intelligent, perceptive and sensitive. At the time I was touched by his concern. It was certainly as genuine, I am convinced, as the connection between us. And so, all these years later, if a touch of scepticism should creep in about ulterior motives I shrug it off. It really does not matter. I am aware how people in his position, who are surrounded by friends with plenty of money and working in the tourist industry must, at times, desperately crave a way out of their own situation. By whatever means possible. I may well have been a rich widow or, at least, someone who was in a position to help out. I was not either of those, but who would have known. Whilst I was there I hardly ever spoke about myself and my situation; perhaps a little to Sarah and Marie-Therese, maybe also to Ian, but not to anyone else.

This was my very last evening at Utopia. I pushed away the sadness as I wanted to enjoy it. I got into the bar early, about 6.00pm. Rush was there with MK and Ang. They were busy as there were quite a lot of people eating even at that time. Ian came along later. I had bought a bottle of Sang Thip from the supermarket for us all to have later. I shared some 'No Name' with Ian and then Rush suggested I have something different as this was my last night (that word again)! I ordered the Indian anchovy I had seen Ian eat the night before. It was very good. Sarah sat with us and ate something later.

Time seemed to be behaving in its trickster fashion and it very soon got to 9.00pm. MK had finished his shift and usually would shoot off to get a few hours' sleep before starting again. But over a drink we talked about music, dancing and about his holiday in September to Kanchanaburi. Such a lovely guy. I walked with him through the garden to where he parked his motorbike and gave him a big hug. This was my first actual 'Goodbye'. I had to take a few deep breaths as I made my way back to the busy restaurant.

I was sitting in one corner of the bar with Ian, Sarah and Noi, while Rush was working. In his forthright way he asked Sarah how old she was. She told and then quickly deflected the conversation to mention my age. Rush laughed and said that when I was on the dance-floor I looked about twelve. I wasn't sure if it was meant to be a compliment. As the evening wore on different people came up to say goodbye to me and so I grabbed lots of hugs: Ron, Brian and Patsy, Melanie and Dave. I was amazed when Margot, the woman from the New Zealand family who had only just arrived, came up and gave me their address, with a kind offer to stay with them.

During the evening, we drank the Sang Thip between us. Even Ron had a shot to wish me well, even though he said he hated the stuff. Earlier, I had taken a few individual photographs of MK, Rush, Ang and Jim. Now, Noi took one of me with Sarah and Ian and then one with Rush and Ang. Sarah then suggested she take another of me with Rush and so I reckoned I should have a decent one of him out of the three.

At 11.30pm Ian and Sarah gave up but, of course, true to form, Rush suggested we go to Chewang for one 'last' time! Ian had declined the offer earlier in the evening and so it was just me, Rush and Noi. We went to the *Green Mango* and, as usual, it was just me dancing. I bought the drinks and Rush bought the food. Some friends of Rush arrived to sit with us for a time. I was surprised to have a drink bought for me by a very attractive, taller than average, Thai guy who was there with another couple at the next table. It gave my ego a bit of a boost.

Just after that, Rush declared that Noi was bored and wanted to go. When we got into the jeep, he suggested going to the Karaoke bar, still accompanied by Noi. I sang a couple of songs, quite hopelessly and then Rush sang the Thai love song he played at *Utopia* a lot. I had no idea of the meaning of the words but it had such a haunting melody. I had always loved it. Back at *Utopia*, Noi got out and I knew Rush had to take the jeep back to his friend. Like a child never wanting to accept the end, I said I wanted to spend just a few moments more alone with him. Like a wise adult, he smiled, took my hand and said, 'Goodnight Sue and thank you … for everything … and I will write.' I had to concede it was very late.

I must have fallen into bed at 4.30am and set my alarm for 5.30am. What was I thinking? Either I didn't set it properly or I never heard it at all. The next thing I knew Ang was banging on the door of my bungalow. It was 6.30am, a full hour after I was supposed to have woken Jim. How could I have let myself be so irresponsible? Not like me at all. But then who was the 'real' me now? I could not be sure. Things had shifted making everything, especially me, more difficult to get a handle on. And I had only been away six weeks.

I was dressed, packed and out in about ten minutes, feeling terribly guilty as Jim drove like the clappers to get me and two other guys to Na Thon. I think she must have broken all the speed restrictions as she got there in half an hour. I thanked Jim profusely, apologised once more to her, asked her to thank Ang for me, stepped straight on to the Hat Yai bus and proceeded to nod off throughout the whole journey. I was on the road again.

A BRIEF STOP IN HAT YAI

It was 3.30pm when I arrived in Hat Yai. I stepped off the bus and straight on to a tuk-tuk, which took me straight to the *Cathay*. It seemed a decent enough place: very friendly and only 100 baht for the room. I had a quick wash and then went out to explore the streets nearby. It was unbearably hot and humid. I bought a map of Indonesia and then, to my amazement, found the tape that Rush had recommended; the one including the haunting love song. He had written the title and recording artist down for me. I went straight back to my room, showered and put on my only remaining clean shirt. There was a communal rest room downstairs where I spent some time cooling down and writing up my diary. By 8.30pm I was dog-tired and so went up to my room. I lay there in the dark, listening to the tape as I drifted off to sleep.

I slept so well, probably for about 9 ½ hours— no doubt needed after so many late nights at *Utopia* – waking before the alarm at 6.30am. I went to get some breakfast and then around 9.15am went down to wait for the mini bus that would take me across the border to Penang.

MALAYSIA

GEORGETOWN, PENANG

There were eight of us on the bus. I was happy to sit quietly without attempting much in the way of conversation. We arrived in Georgetown, Penang about 4.00pm. I couldn't get a room at the *Swiss Hotel* as I had planned and so ended up in a dorm at the *Hard Life,* which just happened to be over a reggae bar. In the bar downstairs I later got chatting to Shania, who I discovered was British despite what I judged to be a slight Australian accent. She was young but appeared to me to be very self-assured. She told me she was only in Penang for a couple of days and so we provisionally agreed to travel on together to Medan in Sumatra. I suspect I was not her first choice of travel companion, perhaps to do with the differences in our ages, but we agreed to meet at the same place the following day at midday.

I wandered the streets again in an attempt to locate an

Indian restaurant, but ended up back at the *Hard Life*, where I started chatting to an Australian guy who was working in Georgetown. Soon his friends, two more Aussies and an English girl turned up and we talked for a while and then went out to eat. I really enjoyed their company. I was back early, around 8.30pm. I took a quick shower and then went down again to sit in the bar and write my diary. It was late before I got to sleep as they were watching football on T.V. in the dorm. But my earphones blocked out most of the noise as I listened once again to my tape, all the while wishing I was back in Utopia.

At breakfast, I sat with an English girl who had just been to Sumatra. As I listened to her, I decided Sumatra would be my next stop. I knew it would not be so easy to travel there as it might be in Kuala Lumpur or Singapore, but I imagined it would be far more interesting. After breakfast, I went for a walk and headed for the *Swiss Hotel* again. This time I was in luck and managed to get a single room for 17.50 Ringgit. Once settled in, I went down with the intention of writing a letter to Julie but began to feel very hot and dizzy. I went to lie down in my room in an attempt to cool down under the ceiling fan. Once more I drifted off whilst listening to my Thai tape. I woke with a jolt at 5.50pm, realising I had arranged to meet up with Shania and her friend at 6.00pm and so would have no time for a shower.

Despite the rush, I was only a couple of minutes late and, after a quick drink, we went to eat at an Indian restaurant. After my two earlier failed attempts to locate an Indian meal, I decided Shania was clearly better at locating them than I was. As it turned out she was British but of Indian parentage, possibly mixed race. She recommended the Dosa Masala, which was served on a giant banana leaf. It was delicious.

After our meal we went to the *Rain Forest* restaurant and to buy our onward tickets for the ferry across to Medan. Shania was familiar with the *Rain Forest* and I agreed that the atmosphere in the restaurant was delightful. Later, a small aboriginal group played some music especially for a customer, who we later learned was Abigail. She was with a very pleasant Malay guy, a civil engineer by the name of Vincent. Across from us sat an attractive young man, who Shania told me came from southern India. The waiter who served us was half Thai, half Malay. Certainly, in my travels so far, I concluded that, more often than not, Asian faces were quite beautiful.

Shania and I left the *Rain Forest* together about 11.00pm having agreed to meet again there the following day at 8.00am for breakfast. As I drifted into sleep I realised that altogether, after initially thinking Penang was unappealing, I was beginning to like it very much. As usual, that was no doubt because of the connections I had made. Perhaps a good time to leave I thought.

I had requested an alarm call from the desk of the *Swiss Hotel* for 7.00am. It was bang on time, even though I'd anticipated it by waking just a moment before. I arrived at the *Rain Forest* at 8.00 and met up with Shania. We ate some breakfast and then had to dash off to catch the ferry. When we arrived at the port there was a backlog of people waiting there, as we learned that yesterday's ferry had not been able to set off because of engine trouble.

The crossing was likely to take several hours but at least we would be cool during the journey, as inside the boat we knew there would be air conditioning.

INDONESIA

SUMATRA

I was beginning to relax again. Meeting Shania in Penang was a stroke of luck. She had been there a few days already and knew all the best places to go. And we got on well, despite our age difference. We enjoyed our last evening at the Rain Forest restaurant, where there was much singing and friendly conversation. We arranged to meet up there again for breakfast the following morning before heading for the ferry.

The crossing, from Penang to Medan in Sumatra – approximately 500 miles over the Malacca Straits – was very choppy. Fortunately, I was not sea-sick, although many people were, including Shania. Five hours later, around 3.00pm, we arrived into the port of Belawan and were herded straight on to a bus, which took us into Medan. On arrival, already feeling a little delicate, we were met by what could only be described as a horde of touts, who pushed and shoved, grabbing our arms as we tried to get down from the bus. It was very frightening. Perhaps because of this, we weren't thinking straight and so made the mistake of taking a cycle rickshaw to what we thought would be Penang Baris bus station, but turned out not to be.

I stopped several times along the way to this erroneous destination, in an attempt to draw out some money on my Visa card: once from a bank and once from a cash machine. Neither attempts worked. It was hopeless. In the midst of what seemed like chaos, we pondered on the well-documented orderliness of Singapore, which had been an alternative route and both began to wonder if we had made a big mistake in coming to Sumatra.

We eventually found a taxi, which took us to Penang Baris bus station. By a stroke of luck, we were just in time to catch a bus with other travellers from the ferry. We were so relieved to see the other backpacks on the roof of the bus. Yes, another 'comfort' of backpacks I thought to myself, with a sigh of relief. The thought of staying in Medan for the night was too much to contemplate.

The bus journey was classic. Soon after we set off it began raining. They stopped the bus and one of the men lugged all the packs down from the roof into the interior of the bus. He dragged them two at a time to the very back of the bus, where he proceeded to make a huge pile of them in the aisle. In the middle of this operation the poor guy also had to act as window cleaner, de-misting the windscreen to enable the driver to see where he was going.

As the bus set off we found ourselves sitting next to Andrew, Simon and Kim, all university students like Shania. By now I had become used to being the eldest member in most of the small groups I found myself in. I suppose I just accepted it. Happily they seemed to as well.

We were heading for Bukit Lawang, a popular tourist destination 96 kilometres northwest of Medan. The village sits on the banks of the Bohorok River within dense Sumatran jungle. The forests surrounding Bukit Lawang are part of the vast Gunung Leuser National Park, which is one of the richest tropical-forest eco-systems in the world. Its reputation has grown not least because of the Bukit Lawang Bohorok Orang-Utan Rehabilitation Centre, founded in 1973 by two Swiss women, Monica Borner and Regina Frey, with the aim of returning captive and orphaned orang-utans into the wild. The rehabilitation programme was suspended some time ago although the centre is still open as a tourist attraction.

BUKIT LAWANG

After an extremely bumpy bus journey on the uneven roads of Sumatra, we arrived around 8.30pm, totally exhausted. We all checked into the nearest place, the *Yusman* and I shared a room with Shania.

It was at the *Yusman* I had my first experience of washing by mandi, a traditional Indonesian way of washing, very common in rural areas. It comprises a large stone tub of cold water, a scoop and a tap with which to draw the water. You fill it only to the level needed, for either a quick wash or a full 'shower'. Using the scoop, I poured water from the mandi over myself. The initial shock of the cold water made me gasp for breath but, once I became used to it, I found it very refreshing. The water inside the mandi must remain clean and so, when using soap, as I did, it's best to stand back a little. The water then simply ran off on to the stone floor and towards a drain, along the lines of a wet room.

In the evening Shania and I chatted with two Dutch men and an Australian couple, Sarah and Geoff. They were very helpful with advice about my money dilemma, telling me where I could cash some Travellers' cheques.

I had a much-needed restful night and, in the morning, we decided to search out the *Jungle Inn* to have breakfast and also to check whether there were any rooms available. It seemed to be a very appealing place, no doubt designed to appeal to tourists. Shania and I had our photographs taken eating an exotic fruit breakfast, decorated with an hibiscus flower. We sat watching the occasional black, grey and white gibbons, known as Thomas' Leaf monkeys, scampering around just outside. Then we checked into our room. At 5,000 rupiah between us (back then it was about 75-80 pence each), we agreed it was not too bad at all.

We spent the afternoon writing diaries and chatting to Sarah and Geoff. In the evening, we went into the restaurant and shared a beer between us, as well as a few stories about our respective relationships or, in my case, ex. No doubt relaxing with a beer encouraged us to open up, but in my experience revealing even a little about partners tends to be a subject that always adds a little 'cement' to female friendships.

We had planned earlier to eat that night at the *Queens* and so, knowing a little more about each other, headed up there. We met a Canadian woman, Misha, who lived and worked in Bukit Lawang. We guessed she must have been into her fifties and if so, for once, someone older than me. She told us she practiced Shiatsu in return for food from the locals. As if to demonstrate how it worked an Indonesian guy, Budi, came over and she started massaging his back. I must admit it was a first for me. I love the experience of a massage, but watching someone else gave it a completely different flavour.

Budi later gave an impromptu guitar and singing session along with some of his friends. He was an amazing character. He appeared not to have a self-conscious bone in his body, which was a source of amazement in itself. In between the songs they sang, he offered us explanations of their origin. A Scorpio, he was clearly very aware of his magnetism but, paradoxically, extremely natural at the same time.

He told us about a dance party being held at another place and so Shania and I walked down there with him and enjoyed a few dances. Budi himself, unsurprisingly, was a good dancer, a complete gymnast on the dancefloor, whereas my preference is always for someone who moves more naturally, flowing with the rhythm of the music. Still, both Shania and I agreed it was good to watch them all. But then, like good little Cinderellas, we left on the stroke of midnight.

JUNGLE LIVING

We were both anxious about sleeping in our new 'home' in the jungle, little more than a wooden hut built high on a bank above the river. Our first night there proved, for me at least, somewhat unsettling. The bed was comfortable, although the constant humidity made for slightly damp bedding. We lit a mosquito coil and then settled down, trying not to be too paranoid about the unfamiliar noises we heard. On the plus side, the constant rush of the river just below us was delightfully soothing and I soon dropped off to sleep.

But then some time later, I woke with a start. I was convinced that the post at the end of my bed had just moved. Was I seeing things? I had not drunk much at all. There must be something under the bed I told myself. Perhaps a rat? We were very near water after all. Or maybe, when Shania went outside to the loo during the night, one of the monkeys had got in? I heard even more noises before finally, exhaustion overtook me and, despite my imaginings, I fell sound asleep. Early in the morning though, we both woke to more noises. It seemed someone or something was banging against the door. We jumped up and opened it to be met with a pathetic sight. A poor dog with a gaping bloody hole at the back of its head lay on our front porch. It was trembling and clearly in a bad way.

I knew that Shania was frightened of dogs and I was concerned about touching it at all because of the danger of rabies. We eventually managed to gently shoo it away. I had become used to seeing starving and mange-ridden dogs throughout Nepal. There were always exceptions, of course, as with Jim's dogs at Utopia, Pui and NoTail, but generally, the treatment of dogs throughout south-east Asia was very different from ours in the West. I had always found it distressing, as I did on this occasion but, apart from reporting it later, there was little else we could have done.

We were late eating breakfast. Shania went down for a swim in the river whilst I walked into town to try to locate the hotel where I might draw out some money on my Visa card. When I finally found Bukit Lawang Cottages, they told me I could do it there but would have to return at 7.00pm when the manager would be back. By the time I had walked back to our hut and written up my diary I was so hot I decided to join Shania, Pete and Charyn by the river for a quick dip. It was gorgeous and so cooling.

We could not visit Bukit Lawang without seeing the famous orang-utans. We learnt the word orang is Malay and

Indonesian for 'man' or, these days I suppose, 'person'. The Malay word 'utan', originally 'hutan', means 'forest' and so orang-utan translates as 'man of the forest'. Its original use was to describe not animals, but forest dwelling humans.

At 3.00pm we all headed down to the river. First of all, we had to cross to the other side in a boat, rather like a large canoe with an extended prow, which was guided across by a system of ropes. We clambered out of the boat and along with the others, trekked uphill for about twenty minutes.

It wasn't a very long walk and we were walking under the canopy of the trees, but the exertion was enough in the humid air to bring on another heavy bout of sweating; always a problem for me when the temperature begins to climb. Shania may have been affected by the heat but at least she looked pretty cool, whereas I was no doubt 'glowing'. It just wasn't fair!

When we eventually arrived, it was feeding time. From a clearing we stood and watched as two Indonesian guys climbed up a ladder on a platform built between the trees and offered bananas and fruit to a large orang-utan who happily took it from their hands and then sat close by them to eat. Satisfied after his meal, he turned away, swung down from the platform and into the trees. It was an amazing sight. We only saw this one orang-utan on the feeding platform, but when we made our way down again to the centre, there were more of them in quarantine cages. A small one sitting on a fence by the path jumped down and tried to cling on to a girl's tee shirt.

On our return we decided it would be a good idea to wash some of our clothes in the river, which reminded me of my time staying at some of the lodges in Nepal. It seems strange to say, but I really enjoyed it. It felt very primitive and natural, although no doubt the pleasure would soon wane if I had to employ this method all the time. After our chores we went for another swim. From the heat and humidity of the jungle, immersing our bodies in the cool river water was glorious. Charyn, who was British and Bob, a very pleasant young Dutch guy, were sitting by the river. He was eating one of the Jungle Inn's exotic fruit salads. We did the usual thing of swapping addresses with them as they told us they would be leaving Bukit Lawang the following day.

Around 6.00pm, after changing, Shania and I set off to walk the short distance from our hut into the centre of Bukit Lawang. I still needed to return to *Bukit Lawang Cottages* to draw out some money on my Visa card and so I left Shania, having agreed to meet up later at the *Queens*.

I had no problem finding the place again but relief turned to disbelief when I was told that the manager was taking a shower. I suspected he had given instructions that he was not to be disturbed. This time I was not going to budge and managed to persuade the receptionist, whose name was Lindy, to attempt to find him and explain my situation. Luckily, she agreed and, whilst we were waiting for him to arrive, I engaged her in conversation, asking about her and how she came to work in Bukit Lawang. After that, she could not have been more helpful. I drew out about 250,000 rupiah, then about £70. I was so thankful not to have to go into Medan, a place I had come to associate with all things unpleasant.

When I eventually arrived at the *Queens* Shania was there with Pete and Charyn. We ordered something to eat just before Andrew, from the bus, came in. He had injured his leg jumping from one slippery rock on to another one. It was really swollen, inflamed around his knee. I asked Budi if Misha would see him and, although Andrew looked unsure about it, he did go to see her later that evening. Then Bob and Chris arrived and sat with us, making a group of six altogether.

We had a really convivial evening, made more amusing by a conversation with an English guy by the name of Hugo, who was defending the all-male membership of the MCC

(Marylebone Cricket Club). They are the governing body of cricket based at Lord's. It was not until 1998 that they voted to allow women members into their fold and not until 1999 that the first ten, including Rachel Heyhoe Flint, were admitted. Anyhow, back then Hugo may have believed it never should, nor would, happen at all. How wrong he was! Some of his comments were so jaw-dropping Bob and Chris could not believe him. Bob declared that Hugo was the first ass-hole he had met on his travels.

I would place myself towards the introvert end of the spectrum and used to spending time on my own. Despite this, maybe even because of it, ever since beginning my travels, I had come to realise how much I loved this impromptu meeting up with other travellers in various situations and in different places en route. It was like belonging to an extended world-wide family. I chatted with Bob about my decision to travel and what led up to it and he told me a little about himself. Later, Budi and another local guy, who had an absolutely brilliant, deep rich voice, made some music. It was a good evening.

Shania and I left together. As we strolled back to our little hut, the incessant noises of the jungle in our ears, we re-wound some of the most enjoyable moments of the evening. By the time we climbed into bed, it was around midnight, although my small alarm clock showed 1.00am. I had forgotten to wind back the hour since leaving Thailand. We continued chatting as we lay there and the topic of our onward journey came up. Shania said she was very happy to continue travelling down through Sumatra with me. I too was glad about that as it made a pleasant change to have someone to travel with. An added bonus was that, despite the difference in our ages, more than twenty years, we did get on very well indeed.

The following morning, we were up very early, at 6.00am (thinking it was 7.00am) and went down to the river with the intention of seeing the orang-utans again. As we waited we were joined by several gibbons in the tree nearby. We had some breakfast at the *Jungle Inn* but then realised there seemed to be an awful lot of people waiting to go up to the feeding platforms again. We decided to wait until the afternoon when, hopefully, it would be less busy. We returned to our favourite spot, on the veranda of the *Jungle Inn* and wrote our diaries until about 3.00pm before setting off again. It was a little cooler than the previous day and so an easier climb. We actually saw two orang-utans this time, one a mother with a baby and I was able to take some photographs of them.

When we got back down we decided to have a go at tubing

on the river. It had to be explained to me: basically, you sat inside a very large inner tube with a net fixed to the bottom and launched yourself into the river. There were four of us to begin with: myself, Shania, an English guy and Joe, who was Irish. We walked up to *Akira* to set off on this quite risky venture. At least that was how I perceived it and I was beginning to feel anxious. The three of them seemed so enthusiastic though, I refused to be the only one to dip out.

The experience itself of tubing on a fairly fast flowing river was thrilling. Even though you set off at about the same time, once in the river, everyone goes their separate ways as the water carries each of you on a different course. A scary moment came when we had to negotiate the rapids but, more from luck than good management, I survived. However, to the extent that I could steer at all, I had intended to 'get off' at the *Jungle Inn* but I was up ahead of everyone and shot past the landing place. I floated on downriver and suddenly realised I was into the town. So I paddled over to the side and more or less fell out of my giant tube, slipping and sliding over the rocks.

All of this 'carry on' was witnessed by two or three village women who just happened to be washing at that very spot. I had unwittingly rocked up in their 'bathroom'. They were very gracious about it. Their smiles and chuckles told of amusement rather than annoyance. Once on dry land, I then had to hike back up to the Jungle Inn, dragging the giant inner tube in my wake. Ah well, I did it. That alone I believed deserved a pat on the back. I returned to our hut, changed into some dry clothes and waited for Shania to return. She had been the hero, having rescued Joe when he popped out of his tube. She was feeling rather battered.

Very soon though I realised I was extremely exhausted: perhaps, the physical and emotional stress combined I thought. But then I began to feel quite nauseous. We went down at 7.15pm, with the intention of going to watch the orang-utan video at 8.00pm. I ordered some food, as I hadn't eaten very much since breakfast and told Shania to go on without me. I found I just couldn't face much of it and so later, went back up to our hut. I sat on a small bench on the veranda listening to my Thai tape, reminiscing about Rush and my time there. Down at the Jungle Inn they started playing music so loud it drowned out my own. I tried lying in the hammock but could not quell the queasy feeling in my gut. By 9.00pm I had to dash to the loo to throw up. I felt terrible.

By the time Shania arrived back at 10.00pm I had been sick again and felt lousy. Despite the late hour, I lay on the bench outside our room as it was so much cooler there. I also didn't want to disturb Shania too much. I stayed where I was until way into the night and when, eventually, I went inside to my bed, was forced to get up twice more to dash to the toilet to throw up. In the morning I still felt pretty bad and took up my position again on the bench outside our room. Shania looked after me very well, wiping my face with a wet towel. She was very sweet. It was comforting to be with someone like her. It awakened in me child-like feelings of warmth and being protected, something I had not experienced for a long, long time.

The following day when I woke I still felt terrible. I spent the whole day just lying or sitting on the balcony outside our room, listening to my tape and dozing on and off. Eventually, I managed to get a Sprite drink down me and later I fancied another.

During that day I did little more than watch, like a nosey neighbour, as a Spanish girl moved into the room next to ours. About 5.00pm Pete passed by and asked how I was. We told him we would probably eat in *Back to Nature* and so around 8.00pm we headed up there after settling our bill. We also bought tickets for the journey to Lake Toba the following day before meeting up with Pete and Charyn. I realised I could not face a proper meal, but Pete recommended plain boiled potatoes, washed down with ginger tea: not very appetising but it did the trick and settled my stomach. I still had a lousy headache though.

We would have an early start in the morning and so both Shania and I were in bed by 10.30pm. I actually managed to fall asleep quickly, despite having spent the whole day dozing. Around 1.30am I was woken by a noise next door. The Spanish girl was back with a friend— undoubtedly male and, putting two and two together, from the sound of his voice, I guessed it was one of the Jungle Inn guys: the one who had promised to wake us up at 6.00am tomorrow— hmm …we'll see if he does. Anyhow, they sounded to be having a good time. And on her first night here too! That, I told myself, is clearly how you do it.

LAKE TOBA

We were woken at 6.00am by my trusty alarm clock. No sign of Wat-tun. I imagined he was still fast asleep next door. We were packed and off down the road by 7.00am. Just by chance we bumped into Lindy from Bukit Lawang Cottages and she showed us where to get the bus.

The journey was a long one. The seats were not well-padded and the roads were pot-holed. The bus bumped along and we were bounced around suffering from the shock of regular painful landings. Luckily, we were still not fully awake and I imagine it must have looked quite comical, like drugged puppets being bounced all over the place. We were thankful to stop for lunch in Berastagi and finally arrived on Samosir Island, Lake Toba about 6.30pm.

Lake Toba, the largest lake in South East Asia, and the deepest in the world, was formed 75,000 years ago after an earth splitting volcano eruption. It is the largest and deepest volcanic crater lake in the world. It is 906 metres above sea level with an average depth of 450metres. Samosir Island is in the middle of Lake Toba and connected to the mainland by a small isthmus.

We headed straight for *Lekjon Cottages* and managed to get a decent room with a mundi for just 5,000 rupiah. It faced directly on to the lake and was much roomier and lighter than our room at Bukit Lawang and for the same cost. It was Sunday and we had already booked the bus for the onward journey on Thursday to Bukatinggi, which meant we would spend three nights in Lake Toba, then a night in Parapat before catching the bus again at 6.00am.

We had agreed to continue travelling together, which I was happy about, except everyone (mainly the local lads) tended to take me for Shania's mother, which I suppose for both of us was not ideal. But then I supposed it was not such a bad thing for me at least to be reminded of the difference in our ages from time to time.

After taking our breath away in a cold mundi shower, we went down to eat. I was not fully recovered and the food was still not to my taste, unfortunately, so I ate very little of mine. Shania was also not able to finish her fish. She went upstairs to read about 10.30pm whilst I stayed to write up my diary. One of the restaurant guys attempted to interest me in a motor bike ride with him the following day— for 20,000 R. No thanks, I told him politely.

Much of the following day was a complete non-starter for

me: still feeling sickly and tired I did little all day. Around 5.00pm I ventured out for a walk. It was still very hot and so despite the hour, I got a little burnt. After a shower though, I began to feel much better. Shania had been for a swim in the lake, which she enjoyed, although I did not fancy it at all. Rivers, streams, lakes: it seemed to me they were all in the same 'open water' category. I was still suffering the ill-effects of my river experience in Bukit Lawang.

But I was slowly returning to 'normal' and that evening we both enjoyed a delicious pizza at Boruna, made by Bronte, yet another Indonesian Scorpio. He was very laid back and pleasant to talk to. Not a bad end to a fairly non-descript day. I reminded myself too that our room was just perfect: light and airy, with seats on the balcony overlooking the lake.

The Batak ethnic group inhabiting the interior of North Sumatra is divided into six sub-groups: the Toba, Karo, Pakpak, Simalungun, Angkola and Mandailing Batak. While two subgroups have converted to Islam, the others have mostly converted to Christianity, primarily influenced by Dutch and German missionaries. The Toba Batak is such a group although ancient beliefs, rituals and customs are still part of everyday life for villagers.

The following day, we hired a couple of bicycles and rode

to Tomok, an ancient Batak village, where we stopped for a drink and wandered around some souvenir stalls. All of them appeared to be in competition selling the same things. Sidabutar was the ancient ruling clan in Tomok. One of the main attractions in Tomok was the tomb of the Sidabutar kings. We paid 10,000R to view sarcophagi, housing kings of the Sidabutar clan. They were arranged in a row, along with several smaller ones, presumably containing the royal children. It was a bit of a disappointment.

The traditional Batak houses were very interesting to see with their curved roofs. The highest point of the roof is at the back of the house, which looks over the lake. The houses themselves are raised and supported on large wooden piles of one to two metres height, meant to avoid floods and wild animals.

The largest, and most prominent, house in Tomok was the communal meeting hall and that of the chief, distinguished from the others by its decorative floral and foliage drawings in red, white and black on its gable. We were told that the three colours represent the three spheres of the cosmos: red, symbolizing the human world; white, made of chalk, for the good spirits and black made of charcoal, representing the underworld.

We continued on our bikes to Ambarita, really a very pleasant ride along a narrow strip of fairly straight road. Here we got to see the real Samosir, very beautiful and unspoilt.

We arrived back in Tuk-tuk around 4.00pm and headed for the little bakery owned by the Australian woman, where we enjoyed a cheese salad sandwich each. I stayed chatting to a Swiss girl, Claudia, whose boyfriend was a Nepalese guide. She was heading back there to see him again. Shania went off for another swim in the lake and just avoided being mown down by one of the ferries. We agreed we had both experienced a few 'near misses' whilst travelling but so far, had escaped unscathed.

Later that evening we ate at Boruna again, although I didn't have much appetite and settled for chips and some of Shania's spaghetti. Just a little but it was delicious. Later we stopped for a coffee at Samosir Cottages, where we met up with Dan, Joe and Gemma. Later still, we all joined in a jam session with some Germans and a couple of Indonesian guys from the restaurant. One of them, Batu, had a withered arm but still played the guitar brilliantly, as well as having an amazing voice. I joined him in a rendition of *Bridge Over Troubled Water,* which I loved. Which probably calls into question my earlier assessment of myself as an introvert if I loved singing in that way? Which I know I do. Hmmm …

complicated! But then, that's nothing new in my case! Best not to question it too much. One has to be adaptable in order to survive. That's my excuse. It was pitch black as we made our way back to our room at 11.30pm.

The following day we ate breakfast before catching the ferry for Parapat at 1.00pm. We had intended checking in to *Charlies* and then returning to Tomok to see a Batak festival but then we realised we would not make it back there in time. We got a room with shower for 8,000R which was fine, although we found it impossible to sit in the restaurant 'rest' area because of the flies. The 'piazza' area outside *Charlies* was really grotty and so it was not surprising it attracted all those flies.

We ended up sitting for about half an hour in the fax place. (This, of course was in the days before mobile or cell phones). I had sent a fax a little earlier to Paul, to let him know my whereabouts. I had already posted a letter to both Julie and Rush from Toba but I had been told they would not go until today.

We found a restaurant up the street where again I only fancied eating chips. No doubt the blandness of the food suited my recovering stomach. We also drowned our sorrows in a couple of beers – probably about a pint each, normally too much volume for me. However, no doubt the alcohol loosened us both up a little and we ended up having a good 'girlie' chat. It was very pleasant. We had come to know each other quite well and I knew I would be sad when eventually we went our separate ways. But for once, we were both in bed early and probably asleep by 10.00pm.

BUKATINNGI

Another early start, rising at 4.45am and, despite the ungodly hour, thankfully we were able to grab a bit to eat at Charlie's before setting out. Forty-five minutes later we were on the bus to Bukatinngi.

We were reasonably comfortable on the back seat, although the journey overall proved to be incredibly tiring. We made a stop once at some hot springs where, to everyone's disbelief, the washrooms had to serve as toilets as well. There was just a gully with water running along its length. Another stop for a passable lunch around mid-day and, something unforeseen, the crossing of the Equator at 5.30pm— a brief stop and that was it.

We arrived in Bukatinngi about 7.30pm and, after checking out one or two places, decided to hang our hats at the *Rajawali*. Even then, we found it a little dim and dismal. We decided we had probably been spoilt by our lovely room at Lake Toba. Even our basic little room at Bukit Lawang was appealing, with the balcony outside and the river flowing below. Gaining some perspective from this comparison, we showered and then went out to eat. By chance we bumped into Dan and so together we all wandered up to the Novatel. All of us were bemused by discovering such a brand in a place like Bukatinggi: just another instance of our naïve eyes being opened to the long reach of capitalism.

Our perspective was not working. The room was not appealing at all. At our request they did change the light bulb. Unfortunately, it was still very dim and, to make matters worse, there were so many mosquitoes, even after their attempt at fumigation, it was not much improved. In an attempt to lift our spirits, we decided to enquire about the onward trip to Jakarta. It was a toss-up between a thirty plus hour bus ride and the Pelni ship which we had been told would take more than forty hours.

We wandered round the market before going back to the hotel and writing out a few postcards. I had given a number of people Poste Restante addresses in Bali so I was hoping that by the time I reached there, they may be some mail for me. Then, because we were so tired as we had not been sleeping well, we both managed to have an afternoon nap.

In the evening, after a shower we ate with Dan again and an English girl, Kirsty, who gave me an address for some teaching in Bangkok. At the time I was keeping all options open for future work and travels. We all enjoyed the rest of the evening watching a troupe of traditional Indonesian dancers.

After another disturbed night, we ate breakfast and went out to look round the markets again. The atmosphere was bustling and colourful and we took a few photographs. We had decided to go by boat but had been told we needed to go to Padang to book the ferry. We learnt this at an information office 'manned' by three young Indonesian women. We knew Indonesia was a Muslim country and yet, so far, we had not had the opportunity to speak with any Indonesian women. These three were softly spoken, sitting side by side at a desk wearing their hijabs as you might expect. They looked so demure. They told us all the basic facts about the ferry and, just as an after-thought, Shania posed a question about the food on the boat. They glanced at each other and then the one in the middle smiled sweetly and said, 'It's bull-shit!' It took only a few seconds for us to recover before the same woman said, 'It's a good idea to take your own food on to the boat.'

We took a bemo to the bus-station and only just managed to get seats on the bus to Padang. It was air-conditioned and comfortable and so during the two-hour journey I nodded off once or twice. A young Indonesian guy carrying a guitar got on the bus at one point. He played and sang a couple of delightful songs.

When we arrived in Padang, we took a functional room in a hotel very near to the bus station and decided to go food shopping for our boat journey. It had to be portable and last for three days. Unfortunately, our only option was bland western food: white sliced bread, cheese slices, crisps, biscuits and, in order to include some kind of healthy option, a very large melon.

We ate Gado Gado at a pavement café area and, after setting up our mosquito nets and a couple of coils, were in bed by 9.00pm. We were up again at 6.45am, although I had not slept well at all. Most of the night there were noises outside the room and the television was blaring away in the hotel. We both had a quick swill in the mandi and went downstairs. They brought us a cup of tea with the usual helping of condensed milk. We paid up and waited for our taxi with a very chatty Dutch couple. The hotel guy was very helpful. He organised everything, including taking us to the Pelni ship office and acquiring the tickets. He even carried my bag containing the gigantic melon on to the boat.

We eventually found Deck 3 and our two berths, each of which consisted of a single blue plastic mattress laid out on a kind of wide bench about half a metre off the floor. We both surveyed the scene and realised there were rows and rows of them, positioned back to back or, more literally, head to head, with a metal see-through grille between each row. Was this what it was like all those years ago in the hold of a convict ship? The floor was very dirty, with scraps of food and bits of paper everywhere. We investigated the toilets, which were just   as bad. Some of the taps didn't work. Where they did, the water just went through a hole on to the floor, so much so that, not too far into the journey, the whole floor of the toilets was awash, just like the bilge of a ship, which I guess it was.

We dozed and ate some of our provisions even though everything was processed and tasteless, apart from the melon that is. We had hoped we might be able to buy a decent meal later, but the food in economy looked revolting: mainly fish-heads we were told and we were prevented from going on to the upper decks, where the first and second-class travellers, possibly tourists, were. Oh, the downside of choosing economy in Indonesia. It certainly brought it home to us what it felt like to be treated like one of the under-class.

At one point during the day we discovered we had been locked in. When I asked why, we were told that they were checking all the tickets. We could not believe it. What if someone were to be taken ill or was claustrophobic, as I could be when feeling 'closed in' with no route out? Of course, I knew more than most the power of the mind and, at that moment, because an escape route was denied me, I really felt the need to breathe some fresh air up on deck. It took all my will power not to begin panicking. Instead, I demanded they open the doors. I was told they would have to check with an officer. At that precise moment we watched as six or eight officers came pouring out of a room. I appealed to one of them but they were not prepared to help.

I have always believed, when getting nowhere in a work situation, that the best chance of at least being listened to is to go to the top. It did not take too long to figure out that in this context that would be the Captain. In one last ditch attempt to get our voices heard Shania and I asked to speak to him. We were escorted to his room/cabin, where he appeared to be relaxing, drinking tea and watching television. He offered us biscuits and Coke. Shania, who you may remember was studying for The Bar, proceeded to tell him that by locking everyone into the lower deck of the ship he was contravening International Law. He did call in the First Officer and had a few words with him but, apart from that, we both concluded he had not taken us seriously at all. We were women after all! We did get to sit up on deck for a while, so we achieved a victory of sorts and to be able to breathe fresh air was wonderful: such a basic freedom that we take for granted until it's denied us. After all the excitement at 9.30pm we finally turned in. I read for a while and was probably asleep by 10.00 and amazingly, apart from a couple of times when I woke briefly, slept right through the night.

I was woken the following morning to what sounded like hymn singing coming from the row of beds just behind our heads. Three Indonesian girls were harmonizing. It was not totally unpleasant, but still a bit much for 6.30am. I decided to attempt a strip wash, despite the less than appealing washrooms. I desperately needed to change my tee-shirt. I felt really hot and sweaty, not helped by having slept on a plastic mattress. Luckily, I was able to lay my hands on my flannel, a relatively old-fashioned item, but useful when backpacking, especially for moments such as this.

Shania and I spent most of the rest of the day on deck. We only had our unappetizing, 'cardboard' food to look forward to and by now we were heartily sick of it. After lunch in the heat of the day we managed to find some shade and dozed for a while. I wrote a letter back home describing our sailing experience and, despite the actual frustration, the words on the page depicted the humour of the situation.

In the evening we went to sit at the back of the ship and chatted for a while to a Dutch couple. It was quite dark by then, the breeze still warm on our faces and above our heads thousands of twinkling stars. It was pleasant: peaceful, yet at the same time a little bizarre. There I was on the deck of a ship in the Indian Ocean in the southern hemisphere, thousands of miles away from every single person I knew. As we rounded the southern tip of Sumatra, in the distance across the ocean we saw Krakatau erupting, belching out flames into the darkness. It was an amazing sight. We sat and watched for quite some time before reluctantly returning to our place in the bowels of the ship to turn in for the night. The toilets were in a terrible state by then. Whether it was the phenomenon of the volcano or thoughts of family and friends back home, my mind would not settle and I found it very difficult to fall asleep.

JAVA

We arrived in Jakarta, the capital city of Java, about 6.00am but were not able to disembark until 7.00. We were very tired, dirty and unwashed. It felt miserable and I could genuinely understand how those unfortunate enough to experience this physical state day in, day out, would soon be depleted psychologically and emotionally.

We took a taxi with six others to Jalan Jaksa and tried to get a room there. A lot of the places were full and a room we looked at was 20,000R which we thought was far too much. We had some breakfast which consisted of very soggy toast. It seemed we could not yet escape our tasteless diet. We decided that we were never going to get what we were looking for in Jakarta and so walked to the train station and caught the next train to Bandung. The train was clean, by this stage much cleaner than we felt, and comfortable, although the atmosphere was very stuffy. We arrived, stepped outside the station and were immediately approached by a guy from *By Moritz*, which was where we were headed anyway.

The room was 17,000R, more than we had ever paid before, but we decided we would take it just for one night.

We were so relieved to be able to shower and change. Our clothes were filthy dirty. It felt great just to be out of them. We then walked to *Asia-Africa* to look for the Braga pub and restaurant, where we had read they served Indian food. We ordered samosas, naan bread, chapatti, mushroom curry and potato curry. It was less spicy than authentic Indian food, but we both agreed it was better than anything we had eaten in ages. As we entered the restaurant it had just begun to rain and by the time we left, the streets were very wet and it was still raining. We wandered around a few of the shops, thought we might try somewhere else for a cup of tea but the place was dead and so we headed back to *By Moritz*.

Bohara, the guy who had met us at the station was playing his guitar and singing. We did a quick change out of our wet things and then sang along for a while. When I turned in at 9.30pm Shania was already fast asleep. Not for me though. It turned out to be yet another restless night. If only I could switch off my thoughts.

We ate breakfast and then went to see about booking our bus for Pangandaran. Our first attempt at trying to phone from the station failed but we eventually managed to do it through the hotel. It would be 15,000R including a pick up at *By Moritz* at 7.00am and then they would take us to wherever we wanted to go in Pangandaran, which happened to be *Delta Gekko Village.*

We caught a bemo from the station to Jeans Street, which was decked out like a Disney fairground and where they were selling copies of brand name jeans and tee-shirts. We ate some gado-gado, cooked before our very eyes by an Indonesian woman. It was delicious. After locating the Garuda office to change my onward flight date from Bali to Australia, we both went into the Asia-Afrika conference museum. It was while we were in the museum that Shania suggested splitting up for the afternoon.

I agreed of course, but inside my initial reaction was to be a little bit taken aback. Not untypical for me when believing my company is no longer appreciated. I was aware of this sensitivity, although at the time, not its original source. Since then I have learnt that when people want to do their own thing it's quite usual for them to want some time on their own, especially people travelling alone, as Shania was. As for me, I was enjoying our time spent together but it was O.K. and good for me once more to have to find my own way round.

I went into a shopping centre and wandered around a few shops. Shopping has never been my 'thing'. However, I did pop into a KFC and ordered some fries before going to the

Post Office to buy some stamps. Back at the hotel I decided to write to MK at *Utopia* telling him all about my travels since leaving Ko Samui. I hoped he would be able to understand all of my ramblings as I wasn't sure his command of written English was as good as Rush's.

Shania arrived just after 5.00 and later on, after we had both showered and changed we went down and sat with Guy and Udian, sharing a bottle of Arik between us all. Then we set off for the Night Market where we ate at one of the stalls. I had Tempeh Kicap a delicious dish made with tempeh, (a soy product similar to tofu) and a peanut sauce. The atmosphere in the Night Market was buzzing and I realised how much I loved Indonesian street food. It certainly knocked our British fish and chips into the long grass. Later we all walked back to the hotel together. Shania went straight up to bed whilst I stayed chatting a while longer with Guy, Udian and a Belgian girl.

PANGANDARAN

The following morning, we ate some breakfast and finished gathering our things together. Downstairs there appeared to be quite a few people waiting for transport from the hotel. Our mini-bus arrived around 7.00am and we shared it with a Dutch couple. Very soon after we set off, the bus stopped to pick up and Indonesian guy with a small child.

The journey to Pangandaran was very scenic: lush, exotic vegetation in-between what appeared to be small villages. We stopped at 10.00am for a quick bite to eat and then we all trooped back into the mini-bus. We were both extremely tired by now. All the non-stop travelling had finally begun to catch up with us.

We arrived at *Delta Gekko Village*, about 4 kilometres outside Pangandaran, at 1.00pm. The place itself was just set back off the beach and was quite amazing. It was set up like a small community with an open restaurant area at one side. We hadn't been there very long when we were introduced to one of its permanent residents. I noticed him as we sat relaxing with a cold drink in the restaurant. At one point I looked up and there, in the space between the tables, dangling upside down from a narrow beam, just above head height, was the resident bat. We were told he was perfectly harmless, but to make ourselves scarce if he should ever turn himself the right way up, as he only did this when he was about to pee.

We were allocated a bamboo hut with a large double bed. There was not a great deal of space but the quirkiness of it made up for that. The bathroom, containing a large mandi and squat loo, was attached and very attractive: the floor made up of small, coloured mosaic tiles, a dark wood framed mirror and buffalo horns for pegs. But the most unusual aspect of the bathroom was that it was completely open at the top to the outside. It took some getting used to but, unless someone took a ladder to the outside wall, it was impossible to see over and into the bathroom. The bedroom led out on to a large porch area with a table, two chairs and a lounger, all bamboo. The porch itself overlooked a quiet 'square', as did two of the other huts, but still privacy was maintained as they were screened off by bamboo and trees.

We christened our open shower area and then decided about 4.00pm to go into Pangandaran as Shania wanted to send a fax and I wanted to buy some sun-screen. There was a motor-bike for hire and we did attempt to master the gears etc. However, without any time for practice, it was far too tricky for either of us. In the end we opted for the other option, a pedal bike each. They were not in the best condition but we agreed the exercise would do us both good.

We stopped for a drink in Pangandaran, while Shania wrote her fax and, by the time we set off back, it was getting quite dark. Not yet accustomed to the instant way in which darkness falls in south-east Asia, we were soon cycling along in the pitch dark. There were no lights on our bicycles, something we should have checked before setting off no doubt. To make matters worse there was only a new moon in the sky. Our limited night vision was the only thing we had to rely upon.

As we got further out and nearer to the beach, bats began circling around our heads. I attempted to dismiss dark thoughts of one of the creatures attacking us or even accidentally getting caught in our hair. We were not even sure if we were on the right road. It was pretty scary. We kept our nerve and stayed close together and eventually the lights of *Delta Gekko Village* came into view. What a relief! For a moment or two I'm sure both of us wondered if we would make it. I believe both of us were grateful for simply being able to take a shower, go to eat and then, later, just sit chatting on our porch. When you sail close to danger, real or imagined, and manage to come out the other side, life's simple pleasures take on so much more significance.

It was rather strange sharing a bed with Shania, memories of childhood and sharing a bed with my Gran or Auntie when I stayed with them. Still, I slept well but could not seem to feel fully revitalized the following morning. I went to have breakfast and chatted to one of the guys from the restaurant who found our failed motor bike familiarisation attempt very amusing. He told me he did the Green Canyon tour, which sounded very interesting and so we thought we might consider that one. Shania and I spent all morning just sitting talking to Junyet, a really pleasant Turkish guy whose wife was Chris. They met in Turkey when she was teaching English out there.

In the afternoon we located the market in Pangandaran without too much trouble and so I was able to buy some Nivea Sun Milk, although only Factor 12, it would be better than none at all. Next, we went to the fax office where Shania has received a short fax from her father, but none from her boyfriend. She appeared to accept it, but I believe she was quite disappointed. I understood the feeling. I too had experienced sometimes bitter disappointment when calling into a Post Restante, anticipating a word or two from close friends or family and finding none. I was aware of how people back home may imagine travelling to be so exciting that any contact with them is perhaps insignificant. In fact, I believe for most people that is not the case. The occasional contact is an essential aspect, providing the reassurance to feel free enough to go into the world, a bit like touching base.

That evening we went to *Bagus* restaurant, where we both enjoyed a delicious fish dish with rice made by Dallin, the owner. He was quite a character. After dinner, he entertained us with karaoke. He told us that his two loves were cooking and singing and he did indeed have a very good voice. Because of the cooking I asked was he a 'home loving' Cancer but he told me that his birthday was August 6th. So, a Leo, like me. I loved singing for sure, but cooking? For me, it's never truly held much appeal. My excuse has always been that from the age of 16, during the years my mother was ill, much of the cooking at home fell to me. I don't really remember but I imagine I resented having to do it.

We took a cycle rickshaw back from *Bagus* and arrived around 9.00pm. It appeared to be very busy in the restaurant and so we went to read on the porch. It was very peaceful and I supposed, for a couple, romantic with the diffused light from the oil lamps. But too dim to read by and so my good old Maglite torch came into play again, this time ingeniously strung up from a washing line just above my book. I had borrowed Erica Jong's 'Fear of Flying' from the library at *Delta Gekko*. I was just getting into it when I discovered about 40 pages missing from the middle, which was very frustrating. I gave up on the book and instead chatted for a while about the role of women in different countries. It was a pleasant end to a good day.

At 9.00am our massage lady turned up. Shania went first whilst I sat on the porch reading and then it was my turn. She was very good. She took a full hour to do a full body massage. She spent the majority of the time on my back and then moved on to arms, backs of my legs and then feet. When she got to my neck and shoulders I realised there was still a lot of tension there— not an unusual discovery for me. Anyhow, we both agreed the whole experience had been extremely therapeutic and, perhaps impulsively, decided to book her again for the following day.

We relaxed a little for a while and then went for a walk along the beach. The sun beat down on our heads and the surf was incredible, with waves at least 20 feet high crashing down on to the beach. We walked until we came to a lagoon. Shania went in while I sat on the side in the sun. We returned to *Delta Gekko* around 3.00pm, picked up a couple of bikes and, despite their having no gears, we enjoyed a comfortable ride into Pangandaran. We called at the Telekom office where Shania picked up a fax from her boyfriend. She was so happy to receive it but sad afterwards as she was clearly missing him. We had planned to try a different restaurant but ultimately did not like the look of it and so we stayed with what we knew and ended up back at *Bagus*. We both opted for a pizza, which was delicious, but were a little disappointed as, on this occasion, our meal came without the serenading.

We arrived back at *Delta Gekko* at 7.00pm, showered and then went into the restaurant. Christina and Millie entertained us with dirty jokes. Shania and I shared a beer and then soon afterwards she decided she'd had enough and went in. I stayed a little longer and then went back to our hut around 10.30pm. I read by the light of my torch for about half an hour until it started really bucketing down with rain. It was great to watch from the shelter of the porch and soon it was wonderfully cool. Watching the raindrops bounce off the floor and the roof of the hut across the clearing was quite hypnotic. Eventually, I went in to bed but sleep eluded me. Thoughts about all the people back home, especially those I'd written to. All of a sudden, the final two lines of a poem I had been writing popped into my head and so I had to get up then and write it out.

We rose about 8.15am, just in time to shower before Mina, the massage lady was due to arrive. I went second again. I was still feeling pretty 'bruised' from the previous day but I felt sure I would feel good afterwards. Afterwards, as it was my turn to pay, I pulled out some notes from a wad in my purse and handed her 10 of them. It was only a moment or two after she disappeared that I realised I had given her 100,000 Rupiah instead of 10,000. I was panic stricken. What a colossal mistake! I dashed outside but she had gone. I felt really stupid and angry with myself. I was very down all morning because of it.

We had decided not to go into Pangandaran and so I spent the whole day lazing around, which made matters worse. All that time to dwell on my stupid mistake. About 1.30pm Shania went to play volleyball. Just then Mina showed up. I managed to get one of the guys to tell her that I had made a mistake in overpaying her. I felt awful but I managed to get my money back. Because she was so understanding I gave her an extra 10,000R as 'compensation'. I felt so much better when it was all sorted out and Mina seemed happy enough.

In the evening there were loads of people in the restaurant for dinner. I sat at a table with Eric and Linda and Shania went to sit with Januy et al. By the time it got to 9.00pm I was very tired. Probably all the energy I'd spent in 'self-flagellation' taking its toll. I retired to our porch to read but then decided to write a letter to my friend Margaret back home. I found myself telling her all about Samui and then felt even more pensive. I realised my emotions were in a kind of whirl, swirling around without any kind of anchor. I did not feel at all disconnected from people around me in the present but I was uncertain about my feelings for certain people.

Since beginning my travels, I seemed to have developed a fondness for quite a few different people and yet, not untypically, it was only the males amongst them that seemed to create this confusion in me. Shania was twenty- six years younger than me. I was definitely aware of that. Even so, because of travelling with her for three weeks and witnessing the effect on her of missing her boyfriend, my lack of connection in that area of my life perhaps was hitting home a little more than usual.

We were up early again the following morning as we had arranged to go on the Green Canyon trip and the bus was due to set off at 8.30am. I didn't fancy what was on offer for breakfast and so made do with a few biscuits. We were all given lifts on motor bikes to where the bus waited at the crossroads. There were fifteen of us altogether and so it was a tight squeeze in the minibus. Four of the Indonesian guys just hung off the back of the bus.

We made a brief stop along the way and then when we arrived at the river we all piled into two long canoes. Ours had a covering above our heads. It was now our turn to do some work. We had to row up the river to the Green Canyon. It took about fifteen minutes and when we finally arrived there were about a dozen boats moored up and lots of people standing around on the rocks, where water constantly dripped from above.

We were wearing our swimming costumes and so decided we would go in for a swim. Linda came with me as the pair of us were less confident than some of the others. We swam about 30 metres over to a big rock protruding from the river, sat there for a while to get our bearings and then went another 25 metres to another rock. We must have been feeling braver by then because we both floated down towards some relatively gentle rapids. It was impossible to avoid your head dipping beneath the water, but it was O.K. I didn't panic. Then we clambered on to the smaller rocks at the edge of the rapids, swam back and sat together on the bigger rocks chatting and drying off in the sun.

When most of our party were ready we all piled back into the two canoes and rowed a little way down river, where we moored the two boats. Here we enjoyed a delicious lunch of noodles and fruit made by Maman and the other Indonesian guys. After our lunch had settled we headed back down the river, but this time it was a race. It was great fun.

We arrived back at Delta Gekko at 4.00pm, showered and then changed. We were both exhausted, probably a combination of the swimming and rowing. Shania had already decided she would be moving on the following day. We had been together over three weeks but it seemed much longer. I knew I would miss her company very much. We both ate dinner with Linda and Erik and then Shania went off to write up her diary and when she returned, we joined all the Indonesians in the restaurant in a singalong which lasted for most of the evening.

Kristina, the owner of Delta Gekko came to sit with Linda, Eric and myself later in the evening and spoke to us about what life was like running the place and the pressures involved, of which no doubt the majority of travellers would be unaware. Still, she maintained a well-run place with a very friendly atmosphere which was the most important thing. I suspect what she was revealing was that, at times, she felt quite isolated, that carrying such a responsibility solely on her shoulders could, at times, feel lonely.

The following morning Shania left at 6.30am and so for the first time in three weeks I was on my own. I ate breakfast and then decided I would cycle into Pangandaran. I couldn't find a bike in the shed and so one of the staff kindly lent me theirs. It was quite comfortable despite the fact that the frame was just a tad too long for my legs. The weather was warm but overcast.

Another reason I was not feeling too comfortable was that my period had just kicked in and so I went on a hunt for some tampons. I eventually found the shop where I had seen some a few days before. They cost me 16,000R. After all that effort I needed a rest and so went for a coffee at Bagus. He asked me why I was on my own and where was Shania. I told him that she had gone. Then he asked was she my daughter. I smiled resignedly, opened my wallet and showed him a photograph of Julie, who in fact was only two years older than Shania. 'She's very beautiful,' he said, 'just like her Mama.' Flatterer!

The following day, feeling a little disconsolate, I decided I would give into my lethargic feelings and spend a lazy day. For some reason I began walking along the beach into Pangandaran but it was such heavy going I soon returned to Delta Gekko and picked up a bike. By contrast to the previous day, this particular bike was so small I was forced to ride really slowly, which was very pleasant. What perfect synchronicity, I thought to myself, almost as if my mood and the bike I was riding matched perfectly. The moment I arrived in Pangandaran it began to rain. I went into the nearest restaurant and for a while sat chatting over coffee to a German guy, Bernard. When the rain stopped I cycled along to the market, bought a few things and then went back to Bagus and enjoyed a pizza for lunch. Soon Kath and Micky, who were also staying at Delta Gekko joined me

It was around 3.30pm by the time I set off back for Delta Gekko. I showered and then read for an hour before dinner, which comprised of a fish buffet as well as the usual vegetarian food. Over dinner we were all entertained by a Sudanese dancer and a martial arts display, accompanied by a traditional band of pipes and drums. I sat next to one of the Indonesian guys, who appeared to take a fancy to me, although the feeling wasn't at all mutual. Despite the fact that I found some Indonesian men attractive, this particular guy was not one of them.

Although later he got me up dancing with a yellow scarf, a particular Indonesian tradition. I really enjoyed it. Later still, we all went on the beach, where they lit a bonfire, played guitars and sang. It was great fun. Unfortunately, I didn't get to bed until 1.30am, which was not a good idea as I had to be up at 5.30am. What is it about last nights, when all my sense of time disappears? Or is it that, in my desire to hold on to people and places I have loved until the very last minute, my wish not to have to say goodbye, all my common sense disappears?

Memories of my last night at Utopia returned: Rush's protectiveness, dropping me off but refusing to sit with me on the balcony and, because I overslept, Jim's mad dash in the morning to get me to the ferry in time.

YOGYAKARTA

I had done most of my packing yesterday and so when I woke about 4.45am thankfully I did not have that much to do. I was in the restaurant by 5.30am, before anyone else. I paid Kristina, had a cup of coffee and three small bananas for breakfast and then I was away in the minibus by 6.15. We arrived in Kalipucang, from where we were to take the public boat to Cila Cap, before 7.00am.

I had been looking forward to the journey but the boat was so crowded and I was so tired, I virtually slept sitting up during the whole of the four-hour journey. We stopped for lunch about half-way, which was a welcome relief and eventually arrived in Yogya about 5.00pm. But because people had to be dropped off along the way we didn't arrive at our destination until about 6.30pm. We were taken directly to *Dewi Homestay 2,* which would not have been my first choice but I decided it would do for a night or two.

I went out for dinner with Ed and Helena a young, very pleasant, typically English couple, just out of university. The restaurant was just around the corner from where we were staying so, as I was still very tired, that suited me too. They had told me that they were thinking of visiting a Batik place the following day. I was not sure that was something I wanted to do, that is until we met up with the Batik man himself, who just happened to be dining in the restaurant. His name was Edy, probably assumed, or altered slightly from the original, for the benefit of tourists. His English was very good. Not to mention the fact that he was probably the most strikingly attractive man I had ever seen. He was taller than the average Indonesian and wore his black hair to his shoulders. A deep rich speaking voice completed the picture. After meeting him I decided the trip out seemed very appealing.

I slept soundly that night, woke at 7.00am and after showering, felt more myself again. I walked to the restaurant round the corner for breakfast and then afterwards set off with Ed, Helen and Edy's brother (nice, but nowhere near *as nice*) to the Batik gallery. It was a bit of a tourist magnet. There were hundreds to choose from and in the end I bought a couple of traditional designs, one for myself in gold and a red one for a present. The three of us carried on together to the Post Office, where I picked up some details of the Ramayana Ballet, which I really wanted to see.

I left Ed and Helen then and as I wandered round the shops on Jalan Marliboro, bumped into the Dutch family I'd met in the Green Canyon. They were staying in the south of Yogya and said how nice it was there. Earlier I had spoken with a French woman who had said the exact same thing. I took that as an indication to investigate. I caught a bus to the area and looked at a few places. As luck would have it, as I was walking around the area, I met the other Dutch couple, Loek and his wife, who were staying at the *Muria*. They encouraged me to check it out and so, there and then, I went to look at a room. I snapped it up as both the guest house and the area are much more appealing and, for a slight increase in rent, breakfast was included too.

I returned to *Dewi Homestay*, then went straight out and bought a few things: a wrap-around skirt, a tee-shirt and a new sarong. I had left my lovely Samui sarong in my room at Pangandaran, which I was sad about. I had taken photographs of me wearing it there but I find that being able physically to touch an object, or item of clothing, brings an extra dimension to the memory. Still, I was feeling much better about being in Yogyakarta.

In the evening, after an early dinner, I celebrated by treating myself to an ice cream and cup of tea at a local restaurant. There I wrote up my diary and a few postcards to send to friends and family, lingering longer than usual as I was reluctant to return to what, to me, was quite a dismal place. I was looking forward to moving to the *Muria* the following day. With what I'd seen with my own eyes and the recommendation from Loek, I was sure I would feel happier there.

Eager to make my move, I was up early the following morning and headed out for breakfast at 7.30am. As I walked to the restaurant Shania passed me in a bus on her way to Bromo and shouted out her 'Goodbye'. It was good to see her again. I was thankful that I was in a good place too after the last few days. After breakfast, I paid and then set off by becak for the *Muria.* It was so relaxing, especially since I had the obligatory balcony on which to sit and relax. I realised how much I loved having an outside space or balcony, a peaceful space to sit, write or just think.

After I had settled in I went back into Sosrawijan, made a couple of short phone calls to friends back home, before returning to the *Muria* to relax for a while. At 7.30pm I went out to a restaurant to eat and had a very interesting conversation with an American guy in the restaurant. He was a volcanologist and was monitoring Mount Merapi. He told me he went up there every two weeks to check batteries in the seismic monitoring equipment. It was fascinating but far too technical for me to understand.

No doubt my friendly volcanologist, having no desire to

spread any alarm, as well as realising my ignorance on the subject, kept our conversation to the bare facts. Since then I have learned a little more about Mount Merapi and about what was happening at that very time not that far from where we were sitting.

Mount Merapi, one of the most active and dangerous volcanoes on Earth, sitting 1700 metres high north of Yogyakarta entered a new eruptive cycle on 20 January 1992. In November 1994, the largest pyroclastic flow (an intensely hot mix of lava fragments, ash and gases) in many years rushed down the Boyong, Krasak and Bebeng valleys, causing devastation in the Kaliurang recreational area and killing at least 64 people.

Following the November 1994 disaster, Merapi remained active and in March 1996, the volcano was described as 'very quiet', with low seismicity and no significant surface activity. However, Merapi became active again on 11 August 1996, *just over two weeks after our conversation.*

On that day, I was in Lombok on the Gili Islands and completely ignorant of what was happening back in Yogyakarta, where residents in the same valleys were ordered to prepare for possible evacuation. Luckily, on this occasion, there were no casualties.

BOROBUDUR

On the Sunday morning I sat out on the balcony and breakfasted on pineapple, a boiled egg, toast, banana and tea. Wonderful! At 9.15 I set off for Borobudur. I had only seen pictures of this amazing structure, one of the greatest Buddhist monuments in the world. I have always found much to believe in Buddhist philosophy and being so near, I knew I must see this 9th century Mahayana Buddhist temple in Magelang. The history of Borobudur is fascinating. Although there is no written record of who built the temple, it is estimated the building began around 750AD and was completed during the reign of Samaratungga in 825.

Mount Merapi is believed to have erupted and forced the central Javanese people of the region to flee and for centuries, Borobudur lay hidden under volcanic ash. It was not rediscovered until the time of Sir Thomas Stamford Raffles, who was made Lieutenant-Governor of Java, a position he held from September 1811 to March 1816, during which time   Britain gained control of what was then known as the Dutch East Indies from Holland.

Contrary to his predecessors, the Dutch colonial government officials, Raffles was far more understanding of the needs of local inhabitants and wanted to do the best for them. In 1814, it was likely that a Javanese village chief, encouraged by Raffles, felt able to tell him about the temple ruins.

I caught a bus at the end of the road to the bus terminal and then the public bus to Borobudur. The driver was crazy. The erratic way in which he was driving led me to believe he must surely have a death wish. Given that I was visiting a place of contemplation it wasn't the best start to the journey. We arrived at Borobudur at 10.45am, luckily still in one piece. From there, I took a becak to the temple.

The temple is in the shape of a pyramid and has three major levels, each of which represent a stage on the way to the Bodhisattva ideal of enlightenment. The price of my entrance ticket included a guide. He explained about the stupa: how the carvings round the base described the life of Buddha and how those on the different levels symbolised the spiritual journey. The lowest level, which is partly hidden, illustrates the realm of earthly desires or feeling, the next level depicts the realm of form, or control of desires and the upper level depicts Nirvana, which is above desire and suffering and is the realm of formlessness. It was fascinating. I took a few photographs and, before leaving to catch the bus back, touched the Buddha's foot, which was supposed to be lucky. Later though, I realised I had used the wrong hand! Ah well!

Around 6.00pm, a little earlier than usual I went to Via Via to eat. They had a Javanese dance course on offer but unfortunately, not for another week. However, I did see a poster for a bike ride of 15K to a Javanese Kamping and, as I was waiting to pay my bill, got chatting to an Australian woman, who was also on her own. She too fancied the bike ride so I realised I may see her on the 30th. Her name was Lianne and she seemed very pleasant. She told me she lived in Sydney, gave me her address and told me to look her up when I arrived, which I felt was another stroke of luck. Perhaps the Buddha's foot produced its magic whichever hand you used. I was back early around 8.00pm and spent the whole evening writing a long letter to a friend.

After another restful night's sleep, I was feeling relaxed and so took my time over breakfast. I had to decide about my onward journey. I had been considering going to Solo, a lush mountainous region, 60 kilometres east of Yogyakarta but, in the end, opted for a tour to Mount Bromo. I would stay in a Homestay on 31st July and then the following morning, take the bus and then ferry to Denpasar. It seemed to me pretty good value for £20 and would break up the journey to Bali. I would arrive four days earlier than planned but that wasn't a problem.

  Having made the decision, I went on to Via Via to book the bike trip. They told me that so far there would be three other people, hopefully one of them the Aussie woman I got on so well with. I called back again at 11.00am and then again at 12.00pm to check whether I had received a fax. But there was nothing. Perhaps it was my visible disappointment or just the fact I was beginning to wilt due to the extreme heat but, during my second visit, they brought me some tea on the house, which was very much appreciated.

PRAMBANAN AND THE RAMAYANA BALLET

I decided that I would have a lie down in the cool of my room, before showering and leaving for Prambanan about 3.00pm. I wanted to be in the best frame of mind possible, because I was very excited about the rest of the afternoon. I actually set off from the *Muria* a little early, not an uncommon habit of mine, to catch the bus to the terminal. Once there, it was no problem at all locating the yellow Pemuda bus to Prambanan.

I was going to the ballet. I've always loved ballet and for many years was 'in love' with Rudolph Nureyev. He was so beautiful and such an inspiring dancer, combining grace with a powerful athleticism. I saw him dance in October, 1981 at the Palace Theatre in Manchester. He was 47 then, just a year younger than myself as a traveller. He was probably a little heavier on his feet at that age, but then I had a seat fairly close to the front of the stage, so it was not surprising I could hear each time he landed on the wooden stage.

I was almost as excited to be going to this ballet performance near to the Hindu Temple at Prambanan. As we alighted from the bus we could see the temple, just a walk away, in the near distance. At 70 metres high, it dominated the skyline. There are in fact three main temples, decorated with reliefs illustrating the epic of the Ramayana and dedicated to the three great Hindu divinities or Trimurti: Brahma, the Creator; Vishnu, the Preserver and Shiva, the Destroyer. Most Hindus believe that Brahman is present in every person as the eternal spirit or soul, called the atman. Brahman contains everything: creation and destruction, male and female, good and evil, movement and stillness.

All of this was explained to me by the guide and was included in the cost of 5,000 rupiah. He was very good and quite amusing as he recounted the Ramayana story. After his tour I went to seek out some more film for my camera and bumped into a couple of girls who had been staying at Delta Gekko at the same time as me. Having bought some film I realised I was quite hungry and so bought some Nasi Goreng from a stall not far from the theatre.

At 6.00pm I walked towards the open-air theatre. Seated on the low wall at the front of the tiered seats were two Indonesian guys. One of them walked towards me and, to my surprise, addressed me by name. He explained he worked in the travel agents where I had booked the tickets, spotted me when I arrived and wanted to speak with me.

We sat and chatted for about half an hour. His name was Muji and, in that short space of time, he told me quite a bit about himself. He was 27, one of eleven brothers and sisters, although two of his brothers had died, one at just sixteen, of a heart attack. His father was dead and so he was expected to look after his mother because he was unmarried. He told me he nearly 'made it' once with someone he knew for many years but they split up four years ago, it seemed because her family was rich, whereas he had no money, only earning 75,000 rupiah (about £22.00) a month. She cried and he was ill because of it and had to go to hospital.

When he had finished his story, I was almost crying too. To someone like Muji, I must appear to be rich too and so, to gain my sympathy by telling me his, no doubt genuine, story laced with misfortune might result in some kind of financial contribution. However, it did not occur to me in that moment. I suppose I was used to people finding me a good listener and so I told him I was sure he would find the right person soon.

I was not a stupid or insensitive person, but it was not until much, much later, probably after I had returned from my travels, that the pieces all began to fall into place. I was to realise with hindsight that, on a number of occasions, I had been made aware of similar hard luck stories.

227

I became aware that back then, perhaps still, a woman travelling on her own was quite unusual. In those cultures, I was perhaps perceived by many as someone who was able to travel because I was rich. Though that was far from the case— in fact I would maintain just the opposite— compared to many of the indigenous people I met as I travelled through south-east Asia and certainly through their eyes, I probably was. I decided not to reveal to Muji that, in the partner department, I was experiencing similar difficulties. He gave me his address, I told him I would send him a card from Australia and then we parted.

I moved further up the slope of the amphitheatre and settled myself on the stone seating, still wonderfully warm from the heat of the sun. The three temples provide a majestic backdrop to the open-air theatre. Darkness falls suddenly in south-east Asia and just beyond the open-air stage, the temples were golden: up-lit in the darkness and bathed in light from the full moon above. It was a perfect setting.

The entire Ramayana story, also represented by engravings on the temple itself, originated in India through the oral tradition and is presented at Prambanan in a series of dance movements, accompanied by gamelan music and narrated by a female singer through Javanese song.

The story begins when Prabu Janaka holds a contest to determine who would win the hand of his daughter, Shinta. The story is set in Dandaka forest, where Rama, and Rama's younger brother, Laksmana are pitted against the villain, Rahwana, who soon kidnaps Shinta. At the end of the story, Hanoman, the powerful white monkey succeeds in taking Shinta from Rahwana. When she returns, however, Rama does not trust her anymore and considers her disgraced. In order to prove her virginity and holiness, Shinta is asked to burn herself. When Shinta does not burn, instead becomes more beautiful, Rama accepts her as his wife.

Unfortunately, the storyline is dismally familiar and, for a woman such as myself, depressing. However, the actual performance as an art form was wonderful and could be appreciated as such. The gamelan music was appealing, the costumes amazing and the dancing spectacular, as were the acrobatics and special effects such as a fireball game, depicting the attempted burning of Shinta. I managed to take about fourteen photos before the battery ran out on my camera. This was, of course in the days before mobile phones.

As I was leaving I noticed to my surprise that Lianne, the Aussie girl I met in Via Via had been sitting in my row. She confirmed that she was one of the five who would be going on the bike trip tomorrow, which I was very happy about. There was no problem at all getting a bus back. It dropped me off at 10.00pm and, ever hopeful, I called in at the Wartel place to check if Paul had sent me a fax. But I was out of luck.

The following morning those of us going on the bike trip, including Lianne, all met up at Via Via. We cycled through four different Javanese villages and then called in at one of the local schools. The children were very young, probably between six and eight, all wearing big smiles for the cameras. It was great to see 'behind the scenes' into the real lives of the local people. As the sun rose it became hotter and hotter and, by the time we arrived back, even though I had on sunscreen it had still caught a little on my face and shoulders. I hadn't partaken in any proper exercise since my Annapurna trek and, after cycling all morning, it seemed as though all my bones were aching.

Unfortunately, in the afternoon everything seemed to go downhill. It all centred around my camera playing up which, in the end, proved very frustrating. I had put in a new film to take pictures at Borobadur. I had only taken four when the camera wound on of its own accord. I had to then rush off to get another film as I knew I would want to take pictures of the ballet. And so on this afternoon I went out to buy another battery as the previous one had packed up after only fourteen photos at Prambanan. But it wouldn't work. I made the mistake of opening the camera and pulling at the film and realised I had probably ruined all the beautiful shots I had taken of the Ramayana ballet. I could have kicked myself.

At 6.00pm though, everything had calmed down and I was thinking ahead. I had packed most of my backpack in readiness for a fairly early start tomorrow. At 8.00am I would be picked up from the hotel, which was a great relief not having to tramp off somewhere carrying a heavy pack to catch a bus. From there it would be on to Bromo, where I knew everything would be organised. As an independent traveller I was used to organising everything myself. It happens to be part of the appeal but, just occasionally, having a day or two organised for you feels like a luxury and is a welcome break.

I set off for Via Via at 6.45pm to meet Lianne, who was already there and waiting for me. We had a really pleasant evening and chatted about all manner of things. I discovered she was a Leo, just like me. Two cool cats together! No wonder we got on so well. We left about 9.00pm and walked to the Wartel together. Still no fax. What were they thinking back home? In an attempt to stifle my Leo 'arrogance' and 'deign to excuse them' I considered they may even be away.

Anyhow, I felt lucky to have met Lianne and realised she would be a good first contact for when I arrived in Sydney. I hoped too there might be someone in her circle who could ease   the way in my pursuit of the essential temporary job whilst I was there. That would be a bonus.

The 31st July, exactly fifteen weeks, almost four months, since I boarded the plane for New Delhi at Gatwick airport. I could not believe it. I had been to so many different places, seen so much that was new, not to mention the many, many people I had met. During that relatively short period living, or at least time, seemed both to have been compressed, whilst at the same time elongated. The sensation, both physical and psychological, was a complete paradox.

MOUNT BROMO

I was picked up by the bus at 8.00am, on the first stage of my journey to Mount Bromo, although we did not actually leave Yogya for another hour and a half. The bus appeared to be going round in circles as it stopped to pick up other passengers. We reached *Bromo Homestay* in Probolinggo around 9.30pm. The journey itself was not the most comfortable: that, combined with the length of time we were cooped up on there, meant everyone was just so relieved to be getting off the bus by the time we arrived.

One positive aspect of being together on a bus for so long is that, if you get on with the person you are sitting beside, there is sufficient time to get to know each other. I met Marcia, a Brazilian young woman, aged 35, a business consultant back in the real world. We discovered we had a lot in common. As we were both heading for Kuta after Bromo, we agreed it would be a good idea to share in Kuta for the short time we would be there.

There was a knock on my door at 3.00am but I was already awake as I had set my alarm   for just before then. We all headed out at 3.30am, clambering into a minibus, which took us part of the way. This was from where we were to start the walk up to the top of the volcano. I have this thing about walking where, in order to keep up momentum, I need to go at a certain speed. If I'm with someone and we fall into step that's great but if, for some reason our steps don't match, I prefer to walk alone. (As I was writing this, I experienced an 'aha moment'. I realised that my preferred mode of walking could well be a metaphor for the way I have lived my life!)

And so too on this occasion, I ended up walking alone for most of the way. It took about an hour of steady, but not too strenuous, climbing. Energy levels for everyone, including myself were no doubt lower in the wee small hours, especially such after a lengthy and totally uncomfortable bus journey combined with only a few hours' sleep. Despite all that, walking along with many others in such unusual surroundings, in relative darkness but lit by the full moon, brought a surreal but fascinating element to the whole experience.

After the long climb, but before reaching the actual cone of the crater, we had to walk across the 'Sea of Sand', a massive flat area of about 90 square metres, more accurately known as the Tengger Caldera. This caldera formed over 250,000 years ago, after the collapse of the top half of what is known as a stratovolcano, or composite volcano: a conical volcano built up by many layers or strata of hardened lava, tephra, pumice, and volcanic ash. The lava flowing from stratovolcanoes typically cools and hardens before spreading a great distance.

The Tengger Caldera has been protected since 1919. The Bromo Tengger Semeru National Park was declared a national park in 1982 and Bromo has been frequently active since historical records began in 1804, with a total of over fifty eruptions being recorded up to the present date. Due to its location on the base of a steep-walled caldera, it generally only poses a local threat to life during explosive eruptions, which may occur with little warning.

Although I was blissfully and naively unaware of it at the time, Bromo had erupted just sixteen months prior to my visit, on 3rd March 1995, producing ashfall 20 kilometres away. And in June 2004, in another eruption, two people were killed and at least five injured. The two men - one Indonesian and the other from Singapore - were hit by hot rocks expelled from Mount Bromo.

When I finally climbed the stairs to reach the very peak of the volcano cone it was 4.40am. It was an amazing and completely 'other worldly' place to be, sitting up there on the edge of the massive crater, whilst the volcano continued to spew out its sulphurous smoke. I stayed in my spot until just after sunrise at 5.30 am. The sky was a brilliant red and orange, a spectacular vision which, unfortunately, I could not capture because of the problems I had been having with my camera. I consoled myself with the thought that on occasion, this being one of them, just staying in the moment and witnessing every small change as it took place was probably a more fulfilling option.

Afterwards, I began the long walk down away from the volcano, across the Sea of Sand and down the slopes, back to where I started out. Many people chose to ride back down on horseback. It was a wonderful sight to see. We all took the minibus back to Bromo Homestay at 7.00am and arrived, weary but hungry, just in time for breakfast. Although I had seen Marcia only briefly as we approached the volcano, we sat together for breakfast. Ari, the guy who had knocked on my door to wake me last night was there. He touched my arm and smiled in greeting as he walked past the table where I was sitting, just as Rush had done on the evening of his return to Utopia.

BALI

We set off again on the bus to Kuta soon after breakfast, which included a ferry trip towards the end of the journey to make the hop from Java to Bali. We arrived in Kuta at 10.30pm. Both Marcia and I were absolutely shattered, but we trudged round Poppies Gang looking for a place to stay. With not a lot of time, or energy and as we were sharing, we plumped for *Arena Bungalows*, a little more upmarket than I would normally have chosen. We dumped our packs and went out to eat at an ungodly hour in the only place open: the appropriately named *Mama's Place*, a German run restaurant. Suitably fed and watered, we dragged ourselves back and showered.

This was when I was taught another lesson to add to my travelling notes. It came about because Marcia jumped in the shower first. I could not see her but I could hear her from the bedroom. What was that noise she was making? She explained later that whenever she showered, she never allowed any water to enter her mouth as she did not trust the water quality; especially in some of the countries she had travelled through, maybe even in Brazil. Who knows what water borne diseases might be spread in this way! What did

I hear that so intrigued me? It was simply the noise of Marcia spitting fiercely every few seconds, whilst the water rained down upon her. It became a habit I adopted too. Why not? We both fell into bed about 1.00am, suitably sweet and clean and … safe from bacteria.

It was a short-lived, typical travellers' relationship, as Marcia left the following morning at 6.30am. I stayed in bed for another hour before getting some breakfast and visiting the Post Office. On finding no mail, I consoled myself with the fact I had told everyone I would not arrive in Bali until 5th. I then went to cast an eye over the beach, which was not as crowded as I thought it might have been. Next, some necessary shopping: sunglasses, a bikini and a dress, so I would be set whenever I do get to a beach. I got back around 5.00pm, still experiencing extreme weariness, not surprising as I had been awake the previous day for twenty-two hours. I took a shower, experimenting with the requisite spitting technique and then dozed for about an hour. I almost decided not to go out to eat, as I was feeling sick and quite depressed.

But rather than allowing myself to sink into the Slough of Despond, I changed my mind and went out about 8.00pm. I had learnt that typically, for me at least, feeling low was usually a sign I needed to make contact with family or friends back home. I decided I would try to ring Paul 'collect' but first went for something to eat: just a light meal before heading off to find the Wartel. I should have staved off my hunger because when I arrived at 9.15pm, I was told that they would not allow 'collect' calls after 8.00pm. I felt really sick and frustrated. I decided I would just have to leave tomorrow without having made contact with anyone from home. I felt so isolated.

Anyhow, as luck would have it, on my walk back to the hotel, I spotted a collect call place and so I rang the Duck. It cost me 5,000 rupiah but it was worth it. I only got to speak with Nick, the receptionist, but it was lovely to hear a familiar voice. He told me that Paul and Steph were away in France, but that Julie had received my fax. I stressed how much I needed to hear from everyone and told him I would be in Bali until the 28th. He assured me he would get on it. I arrived back at Arena Bungalows at 10.00pm. I felt so much better. I had just over three weeks left now in Indonesia and so I decided I would forget about the post until I returned on 25th a few days before my flight out to Sydney.

UBUD

It took only an hour to reach Ubud on the shuttle bus and we arrived at 2.00pm. It felt like a really delightful place. I knew that Ubud was the cultural centre of Bali and certainly it resembled more of what I had imagined it to be than the more tourist atmosphere of Kuta.

I found a room for 10,000R. It was very clean but later, whilst exploring I decided to move to another one tomorrow. *Donald Homestay* – perhaps some bizarre Scottish connection - a little more at 13,000R but it was quieter and in a very pretty garden. There were only three other bungalows besides my own. I had a sense of needing my own space. I called into a café in Monkey Forest Road for a bite to eat. Later, in the evening I went to the Temple to see a Legong dance, traditional Balinese dancing.

It was a fairly early finish and, on my way back, I stopped to look at some postcards and started to chatting to Suzi, an American girl. I decided to ask if she wanted to go for a coffee, something I would never normally ask of a stranger back home. We got to know each other a little and agreed to meet for lunch tomorrow and possibly to go to see the Kecak Fire and Trance Dance together tomorrow evening.

I moved to *Donald Homestay* at 9.00 am the following morning. Unfortunately, I really did not like the look of the place after taking a closer look. The bathroom seemed to be dripping from every orifice and the room itself seemed cold and bare. The people staying in the other three bungalows are French, two taken by one family. It seemed that perhaps my unsettled state of mind and the way I was feeling was affecting my decision making.

I explored a little in the morning and met Suzi at 12.30pm for lunch. We spent the afternoon wandering round the shops, not my favourite pastime, but I did need to add to my wardrobe. I bought a long dress and a sarong. I also went a little crazy and bought a beautiful batik wood mask. It cost 30,000R, about £8.60, so not too bad. It was far too big to carry and so I thought I would look into sending it in a parcel, along with a few other things, home from Bali. We decided to leave the kecak until the following evening as were both very tired. Instead, we met up later and went to *Murni's,* a very attractive restaurant on three levels, with the most amazing carvings and decorations.

I went back to *Lastri House* with her and asked them if they had a room. Another room, although this one would be less than the one at Donald's, except I knew I may not get the money I was owed from them. Still, I reckoned it was worth it to be in a better place.

Back at *Donald's* around 11.00pm I put up my mosquito net. The two French girls in the bungalow next to mine were so noisy, my pillow was like a rock and, although I was very tired, I probably didn't get to sleep until about 12.30.

I woke around 7.00am, had a shower and then went to tell the woman in charge that I would be leaving. As I thought, I was not about to get any change owed to me but in truth it was not much, probably the equivalent of £1. I arrived at *Lastri House* at 9.05am and I was allocated a room. Suzi did not surface until 11.00am and so I wrote up my journal while I was waiting for her. Our first port of call was the bank where I drew out some more cash and bought $150 of Travellers Cheques.

After lunch we hired a couple of bikes from a place nearby for 4,000 rupiah each and cycled to Peliatan. We were intending to get to Mas where they do woodcarving but unfortunately took a wrong turning. Still the ride was very pleasant and it was good to get some exercise. We arrived back at *Lastri House* just in time for a shower and change before catching the mini-bus at 6.00pm for Bona village to see the Kecak dancing.

The Kecak Dance originated in Bona village in the early 20th century. Each year during the period of the November monsoon rains, many of the villagers were struck down by a disease, thought to be smallpox. At least one member of every family would be lost to the disease. The temples were all closed. People could not enter because every family had lost someone, and so the families were deemed to be unclean. With no doctors and with all temples and holy places locked and barred from giving help, making noise was perceived to be the only method left to ward off the disease. In their desperation, their only defence was the hopeless banging of any metal instrument they could lay their hands on: buckets, kettles and cymbals and chanting in a trance like fashion: cak, cak, cak, the word meaning, 'How?' in Indonesian slang. In the Ramayana as well as the Legong dance the beautiful gamelan provides the accompanying music, whereas in the Kecak dance the voice *is* the instrument.

From 1804 to 1974, the colonial Dutch East Indies government and the postcolonial Indonesian state attempted to tackle the problem of smallpox. The vaccination efforts in the colonial era virtually eliminated smallpox by 1940.

Unfortunately, as a consequence of the war, smallpox was reintroduced into the archipelago in 1947. Indonesia finally succeeded in eradicating smallpox in 1974, through campaigns of mass vaccination and surveillance.

As we watched the Kecak Fire Dance in its unreconstructed form and in Bonar village where it originated, I was unaware then of much of its history and so probably not as appreciative as I might have been had I known it. Having just a week before witnessed the Ramayana Ballet performance in all its glory, I believe I was not very impressed. The kecak dancers were all male. The very first women's kecak group was started as late as 2006.

In the bus on the way back I met Hendrich again, the guy I had travelled with from Yogyakarta. I also got chatting to a Swiss girl, Martina and an Indian girl, who worked as a landscape artist in Singapore. Back in Ubud, all five of us went for a meal at the *Casa Luna* and an enjoyable time was had by all. It was very pleasant to be with others in a small group again. Ever hopeful, on the way back I checked to see if I had received a fax from Julie, but still nothing.

Suzi and I chatted on her porch for almost an hour and I finally fell into bed, tired but feeling very relaxed around

1.00am. I slept under my mosquito net and lit a coil. Everything was fine.

I was awoken by Suzi frantically knocking on my door and shouting out that she had to go. For some reason I thought she was leaving at mid-day and last night she had not mentioned leaving so early. I had asked if I could borrow her needle and cotton to mend one of my tops and so that was out of the question. In my haste I also gave her rather too many of my malaria tablets, leaving not enough for myself.

After she had gone I realised this was the third occasion in the short time I had known her where she had been late, or not clear about time and where to meet. I knew I could not travel very far with someone like that. I was aware how lucky I was to have got on so well with Shania in the three weeks we travelled together.

After breakfast Martina, the Swiss girl from the bus, came round. She decided to take what was Suzi's room. She is a very calm, relaxed kind of person, the kind I like to be around. We decided we would go to a couple of temples by bemo, instead of on bikes. The scenery en route was lovely but we both agreed the temples were uninspiring. I decided I had seen enough temples and sunrises for the moment at least. In the evening we went out for a meal with Martina's friend

Anna-Maria, an English girl. On the way back, I bought 'The Horse Whisperer' by Nicholas Evans and read about ten pages before dropping off to sleep.

Another big breakfast from Wayan the following morning— banana pancake and fruit salad – delicious, but I was not used to eating so much so early in the day. I strolled up to Martina's bungalow. She was sitting with Anna-Marie. They were planning to go out by bemo to look at more temples. I had already planned to go into Kuta by bemo as I wanted a black strappy tee-shirt to wear under my new dress. I also wanted to check Post Restante again— ever the optimist!

I managed to get the first bemo to Batubalan for 1,000R but once there. I allowed myself to be drawn in to negotiating a price to take me direct to Kuta with two locals, (Sugi and her husband), which I soon realised was far too much to pay. They were pleasant enough, even invited me back briefly to what was probably her parents' house. They were just trying to earn a living. It was my stupidity in not having checked the exact route before setting off. I told myself I surely should have learnt that much at this stage in my travels.

True to form there was no post, but there were a couple of notes: one from Lynda and Erik and one from Shania, suggesting meeting, but two nights before. So I had missed

247

them. I was so disappointed. I did my bit of shopping, stopped for an orange juice, whilst sheltering from a downpour in Kuta and then headed back. This time the most economical way: first to Tegal terminal, then to Ubung, then to Batubulan and finally the last leg to Ubud. It cost me 3,800R. So that morning I had paid 4,400R more than I need have done. It was only equivalent to about £1.25, which does not sound much but, for a budget traveller, every penny, or in this case rupiah wasted, was very frustrating as I knew I would definitely need it somewhere down the line.

Back at *Lastri House* I showered and was just about to head out to eat when I met Martina and Anne-Marie coming back from their day out. I waited for them and then we all went out to dinner together. It lifted my spirits to be spending time with them and so, when they asked did I want to go to Lovina Beach with them I said I would. They were only going to be there for two days but I would decide on my length of stay after checking the cost and itinerary for getting from Lovina to the Gili Islands, somewhere I had planned to visit. After chatting to Martina for a while I retired with my book.

I slept well, breakfasted at 8.30 and half an hour later Martina and Anna-Marie came round with information about booking tickets to Lovina Beach. I said I would book them as I was heading out to the bank and would go to the Perama office afterwards. To escape the constant drizzling rain, I stopped for a coffee in Monkey Forest Road and began writing quite a number of postcards to people back home. Later, at the booking office I was pleased to discover that I could get a shuttle from Lovina to Bangsal, from where I could then get a ferry to the Gili Islands.

My marathon postcard writing session had eaten away at most of the morning and so, after booking our tickets, it was time for lunch. I had a delicious sandwich in Casa Luna and then went to check on my last fax slip. I was delighted to discover I had received a fax from Julie bringing me up to date with all her news. She failed to mention whether she or Paul had received my letters and so I was left wondering whether they had somehow got lost in the post. In the world before mobile phones and instant messaging, that was the trouble with having only the fax or a letter as your means of communication. On the other hand, life was lived altogether more slowly in those days, which also has a lot to commend it.

I enjoyed my last big breakfast, at least until my return to *Lastri House* on 22nd August. The three of us caught the bus at 9.15am from the road. My itinerary was Lovina for five days, Gili for six, Ubud again for two and then Kuta for three. I made a note to re-confirm my flight from Kuta or Denpasar on Monday 26th August. Moving on again always came with a mix of apprehension and excitement. But this time I would be accompanied once more and, on this occasion, by *two* other people.

LOVINA BEACH

We arrived in Lovina around 1.30pm and it took us around an hour to find somewhere to stay. We were able to leave our packs at the Perama office during our search and so we were literally lighter as we walked. We eventually found a room at *Puri Tasik Madu* to share between the three of us at 24,000R, including tax and breakfast, which meant each of us would be paying 8,000R. Everything was always so much cheaper when sharing.

We spent the late afternoon on the beach. We agreed it was a really pleasant spot, away from the centre of Lovina but near enough to walk in. Later, we ate at *Superman* and had a wonderful vegetable curry. Apart from the company, I was glad I was accompanied by Martina and Anna-Marie as I felt that, despite its attractions, Lovina was not the kind of place I would want to come to on my own.

After our meal we went to another restaurant and listened to some live music. It was not very full and so when Coco, the singer had finished his set, he came over to our table. We invited him to sit and he started chatting to us about himself. He was a Cancer and told us he had always dreamed of becoming a singer. We had a beer and an Arak and coke each and then danced for the latter part of the evening along with a few of the Indonesian guys there. We all really enjoyed our evening.

The next morning we were on the beach for 10.00am. It was very hot. We sunbathed, read and swam a few times simply to keep cool. It felt good to back on a beach once more. I got talking to a little girl who said her name was Julie Ann, although I'm not sure if that was her real name. Many people I had met adopted an English name to make it easier for tourists. She was selling pineapples and coconuts and had her three-year-old brother in tow. She told me her parents worked in the rice fields and that she worked on the beach all day. She couldn't have been more than nine or ten herself. Her boss gave her 200R for every 1500R she made. She also said that when she was not able to sell very much he got angry with her. I told her I would buy two.

Later in the day, about 2.00pm, Martina and I bought two pineapples from Julie Ann, as promised and sat eating them higher up the beach, in the shade of a tree. We were rained off at 3.00pm. Suddenly, I began to feel extremely tired and so I went indoors, showered and then slept for about an hour, after which I felt fully restored. I wore my long black dress with the tee-shirt underneath. It was cool to wear and felt good.

That evening we went out to eat and had a pizza, which predictably was nothing special. We also looked through some tattoo designs. I fancied the idea of having a small one on my back but I knew I would probably not be able to trust a tattooist unless he came highly recommended. We then moved on to another restaurant where there was live music. They were playing James Taylor's 'You've Got a Friend'. Perhaps I was noticeably singing along. Certainly, I must have looked as if I was enjoying it so much I was invited to sing. It was very tempting, as I would have loved to have been a singer, but I declined. Back at the bungalow the two girls retired. I sat on the porch for a while, something I have come to love doing at the end of the day, usually whilst reading my book.

We ate a late breakfast around 9.30am and, because it was raining, did not get down to the beach until about 11.00am. The sun was high in the sky by then and so we sat in the shade. Julie Ann came by, this time without her little brother and I bought another pineapple from her. At 4.00pm it started raining again and so I gave up and walked down to the shops, dodging the raindrops along the way. By 5.00pm I was feeling very tired and so went in, showered and lay down, listening to my Thai tapes, the haunting melodies putting in me a nostalgic mood. The next thing I knew I was waking up and it was 6.30pm.

The three of us all went out to eat a little later at an Indian, although we decided that perhaps Indonesians would be better offering their own delicious Indonesian food in their restaurants. We were all unimpressed with the meal, which seemed fitting, as the whole day seemed to have been disjointed somehow. Yet, as we were passing *Wina* we heard Coco again, this time singing with his rock band. He really had a great voice and he was looking good. We went in, ordered an Arak and coke each and the mood immediately lifted. We took to the dance floor a few times and had a great evening.

When we got back I stayed out on the balcony to write up my journal after Ann-Marie and Martina retired. That evening, Coco, the singer, had looked older than on the previous occasion somehow. That, along with his lovely voice, combined to make him appear more attractive. And a certain mannerism, such as occasionally brushing his hair back from his face, reminded me immediately of Rush. Maybe it was the laid-back lifestyle, the Arak and coke, the music or dancing or all of the above but, as I wrote, I realised how, on the rare occasion, I had found myself drawn to these totally unsuitable and much younger men. It was very frustrating and totally impossible: a clash of head and hormones.

Martina and Ann-Marie had arranged to go snorkelling the following day but Anne-Marie wasn't feeling well. We all had breakfast and then I accompanied Anne-Marie to tell the guy they were not going. We went on to the Perama office where I booked my ticket to Bangsal for Wednesday, two days hence. It cost 30,000 rupiah and I was informed I would have to be at reception for 6.20am in order to leave for 6.30. I would arrive in Bangsal about 4.00pm they told me, but I suspected it would be later.

It was a very clear hot day and we were all on the beach by 10.15am where we stayed until 12.30, when we went back up for lunch. After eating I stayed on the porch for a while reading. The heat intensified and so by 2.30pm we were on the beach again. It had not been since Samui that I had felt the heat of the sun seeping into me. It felt good.

Just then, a young boy, who told us he was twenty but looked about fifteen, came up to Martina and I in turn, asking if we wanted any magic mushrooms. He was clearly well-gone on them himself. He then said that he wanted to 'lie down and sleep with us'. I told him to go and play with someone his own age. Looking back, it was sad really and quite likely that both he and Julie Ann, the pineapple seller, were no doubt forced by circumstances into that situation, having to ply their trade among the many tourists or travellers who stayed temporarily in the place they called home. As budget travellers, we were not rich compared to tourists but, relatively speaking and in the eyes of local people, of course we were. But at the time, we viewed him as a nuisance and just wanted him to go away.

Later, we ate pizzas and, not yet having learnt the lesson about food from another country, found them a pale imitation and not very nice. To make up for the disappointment, we called into another place for an ice-cream. Martina and Anne-Marie wanted to go back early and so we were home by about 10.00pm. They went in to read and I sat out on the porch for a while. Agus, one of the guys from nearby, asked me if I would help him with some English later. I was waiting for him to return when Aan turned up. He had seen us arriving back. He asked could he sit down. It was not very late and I wasn't tired, so I agreed and we chatted or, at least, he did most of the talking. He told me he had had no business for four days. He was twenty-four. His sister owned the Lovina Café and he lived next door to her. He had wanted to be a lawyer and even started university once but had to drop out because he had to work, which he did offering tours and transport to tourists.

Just then Agus re-appeared, a bit mushroomed out. He asked me why I had not been and so I told him I expected him to come to where I was sitting. Together, they talked for a while in Indonesian. Aan explained how he had asked Agus to tell all the guests about his tours but that he never did. It seemed to me there was some rivalry between the two of them. Agus left us about 11.00pm and I told Aan I would have to go soon too but he talked a little longer. Before he left he fashioned a scorpion out of some silver cigarette paper and solemnly presented it to me, gave me a kiss on the cheek and left at midnight.

The following morning, I was on the beach by 10.00am. An hour or so later, I was joined by Martina and Anne-Marie, who had been snorkelling. They were telling me all about their adventure when Aan arrived and asked if I wanted to go and see a marching parade with him. He suggested setting off by 1.00pm and then in a typical foreign and direct turn of phrase he said, 'Go inside and wash your skin.' I had to smile at that. O.K. I told him, but not till 2.00pm.

I had some lunch with Martina, showered and stepped outside just as he arrived at 2.00pm. We drove a short distance and then he tried hard to find a shady spot from where we could watch from his small jeep but in the end we got out and sat under a tree near to where a couple of his friends were sitting.

He told me how much he liked me and perhaps we could be a couple. I said I was far too old for him and anyway, there were plenty of young beautiful Indonesian girls for him to be with. He said they were very materialistic, so who should he be with, a fifteen-year-old. 'You don't understand me!' he protested, at which point he tried a different tack by switching to metaphor. 'If someone wants a mango instead of a pineapple, they are not happy until they have a mango!' I was quite impressed by his determination but could not suppress a laugh and told him I was probably a very over-ripe mango.

After the parade had gone by and having given up on the wooing, he drove me round Singaraja, where he came from and then out a little way into the mountain villages and towards the waterfall. It was lush and very beautiful. He parked the jeep and said he wanted to kiss me. Luckily, there were some villagers across the road looking on with great interest. I pointed this out to him and told him it would be too embarrassing. We were probably parked there for about ten minutes and then I insisted we head back. We stopped once more for me to take his photograph. He wanted to see me that evening but I told him I would be going out with Martina and Anne-Marie as it would be the last time I would see them.

Still persisting, he suggested he could follow me to Lombok and be with me there. I told him it was crazy. And then to try to placate him I said I might see him again when I returned to Ubud or Lovina around my birthday in a week's time, although I had made no plans about when I might return. We might also be in *Wina* or *Malibu* tonight I offered.

That evening, Anne-Marie and Martina suggested watching a video – 'Single White Female' - in the restaurant next to *Wina*. At 9.15 Aan was parked up ahead as we started walking to *Malibu* at 9.15pm. 'Where you go', he shouted. 'Just walking up here', I replied. I was not going to leave the other two and stop to talk and so I guess he may have felt a little spurned. He was a nice guy and so I could not be as insistent as perhaps I should have been. Still, he was exactly half my age at twenty-four and I knew there would be another female traveller arriving soon to take my place in his imagined affections. I didn't know at that stage whether or not I would return to Lovina. It did not matter too much. My mind was already on the next stage of my journey.

I was up at 5.00am the following morning and away by 6.30am. the bus was heading for Padangbai but, with all the marching still taking place, progress was slow and so we arrived late and missed the 10.00am ferry, instead catching the mid-day sailing to Lembar in Lombok. I was very tired. It was all I could do during the crossing to keep my eyes open during a pleasant enough chat with a Kiwi woman, Lou, perhaps in her fifties. She told me she worked in real estate. I knew that Kiwis were famed for their love of travelling but still, it was always a pleasant surprise to find someone older than myself on the travellers' trail.

SENGGIGI

From Lembar we caught a bus to Senggigi and because of the earlier delay, I realised I would have to spend the night there, something not in my original plan. I found a very basic box-like room at the *Patai Indah Senggigi*, showered and then went in search of somewhere to eat. It was late and I was so weary, I had neither the time nor the inclination to check out many of the restaurants and so, when I passed one where three or four guys were just outside for the sole purpose of attracting custom, I hesitated. One of them asked me to step inside. I remarked that it looked too expensive for me. He just smiled and said very persuasively, 'Why not just try it?' He was making it far too easy for my addled brain not to comply and so I did.

He brought me Cap Cay, which I had to admit was delicious and well worth the 4,000R I paid for it. I had a beer, something I rarely did but it seemed that a combination of my fatigue and his persuasive talents, made me acquiesce to his suggestions. As I finished my meal I noticed a couple at another table taking their leave. Now I was clearly a captive audience because I appeared to be the only person left in the small restaurant. The waiter cleared away my plate, returned and asked could he sit down.

We talked for some time about all manner of things: religion, philosophy and relationships. He told me he was Muslim, but lapsed because he drank and smoked. He offered me an Indonesian cigarette to try, telling me they contained cloves, which gave them an unusual sweet taste. He showed me a trick with matches which I could not work out. Like most Indonesians, he was not very tall, perhaps five feet six or seven, but several inches taller than me. He was very charming, with a big smile and very penetrating eyes. He asked had I been on the beach at Senggigi and I explained I had only just arrived and was heading for the Gilis tomorrow.

He told me he would be twenty-nine in November and his other occupation, apart from waiting on tables, was diving. He was a dive master and often went to Gili Air or Gili Meno diving, working for the Blue Coral Diving School owned by his boss, who also owned the restaurant. I told him I would probably go to the biggest of the Gili Islands, Gili Trewangan but would be returning on Monday. At which point he said to be sure to visit him at the restaurant before I left. When I finally got back to my little box room it was exactly midnight.

I was up early and waited outside the hotel by 8.00am for the Perama shuttle. By 9.30 it still hadn't appeared but, while I was waiting, a jeep pulled up and the driver, Eddie, (another improbable English name) introduced himself, before posing the stock questions: what was my name? where was I from and then where was I going? When I returned he could take me all around Lombok on his motor cycle. Maybe. I told him I couldn't be sure at the moment. Eventually, I walked up to the Perama office and caught the bus at 9.00am. Lou, who I had met on the ferry to Lombok, was on the bus. She was heading for Gili Air. With hindsight I wish I had decided to accompany her rather than following my plan to visit Trewangan.

GILI TREWANGAN

On arrival in Bangsal, we had to wait for enough people to make the numbers up to twenty in order to fill the boat, which was the public ferry. I chatted to James from Manchester and his girlfriend from Bristol. The Gili islands are small and so approaching them, we could see all of them ahead of us. They are very beautiful: lush green tropical vegetation, fringed with white sandy beaches. It appeared to be true that, just as I had heard, Gili Meno was the most beautiful. Still, I was heading for Trewangan. Disembarking from the small boat was a new experience, as we had to wade the final few metres. I turned up my trousers but still, managed to get the bottoms of them soaked through.

I booked into *Iguana*, and was allocated a wooden bungalow on stilts, one in a small row of identical ones. Inside there was a mosquito net over the bed, an open attached mandi and outside, a porch with a small table and chairs. *Iguana* was a small complex on a small and very popular island. Understandably, space was at a premium and so the bungalows had been built fairly close together. Consequently, sitting on my porch, with two voluble Aussie guys to one side of me and two Sloane Ranger English girls to the other, was not quite the relaxing experience I had enjoyed in other, more remote, settings. I went out to eat at 7.00pm and watched 'In the Name of the Father', which was showing in the restaurant. I walked along the strip afterwards but after a very short time the line of restaurants dwindled and there was nothing but pitch blackness. I was back at *Iguana* and in bed for 10.30 although, because of the intense heat, found it difficult to fall asleep.

I had breakfast and then was on the beach by 9.30am. It was incredibly hot. By 11.30 I could take the heat no longer and so headed up and off the beach, stopping for a jaffle and cold drink at *Borobadur Restaurant.* I was walking back to *Iguana* when I heard someone calling my name. It was Siba at the Blue Coral Diving Club. He told me he was there for three days. Was that just a coincidence I asked myself? He explained that he was taking a Diving Instructor course and was being sponsored by his boss. He was staying at the Centre and that evening he had to watch a diving video but did I want to go round about 9.00pm to see him. I said I probably would. It seemed to me that spending time alone on these small but beautiful coral islands was more difficult than in some of the other places I had been.

I spent the afternoon on the beach although it clouded over about 4.00pm and so I went back to *Iguana*, showered, read and then dozed for an hour. I went out to eat at 7.00pm and watched yet another film, 'Strange Days' which, not too far into it, I realised I had seen it before at *Utopia*. Neverthless, it was enjoyable.

When it finished at 9.15pm I walked down to the Blue Coral Diving Club, feeling a little anxious as I thought there would be a lot of people there. However, Siba was sitting on the porch on his own. We sat and talked for a while and then he said he wanted to show me his 'place'.

Later that evening, we returned to a kind of loft space, which had to be reached by climbing a wooden ladder. It was peaceful, open to the air and so very cool. Being with him felt really good and natural. I liked him a lot. He suggested maybe we could meet tomorrow evening too. He talked a lot about diving and what he had to do to gain his certificate. The exam was going to be in October, with a mock two weeks before. He was convinced he would not pass because two months was not enough time to prepare. I made a mental note to send him a Good Luck card.

It was 6.15am as I approached Iguana. The sunrise was amazing. It was 17th August and I had learnt it was Indonesia's Independence Day. I stepped inside just before the Australians next door to me began to stir and, from what

267

little I overheard, it was clear they were leaving that morning. Thank goodness. Peace at last. And with a deep sigh, I fell into bed.

A couple of hours later, I woke, showered and was eating breakfast around 9.00am. I didn't go on to the beach until about 10.30am and left around noon. During that time, I went for a swim and a young Indonesian guy happened to be snorkelling nearby where I was sitting on the beach. Never having snorkelled myself I was naturally curious and watched him as he swam around in the shallow waves. He no doubt noticed my fascination because as he made his way out of the water he asked me if I would like to try on his mask. He showed me how to put it on and the correct method of breathing, then suggested I try it out. I made my way into the beautiful turquoise water, feeling strange with the mask on my face but, once in, it was wonderful and much easier than I imagined.

My initiation lasted only about ten minutes but enough to feel confident I could attempt it later in my trip if the opportunity arose. I handed him back his mask and thanked him. I stayed a little longer on the beach and then headed back to my room. I desperately needed to catch up on some sleep and after just a couple of hours I felt much fresher. I showered, read for a while and then went out to eat at 7.00pm.

The restaurant was typically showing a film, probably aimed at unaccompanied travellers like me to watch as they ate their meal. Unfortunately. it was the kind of action movie appreciated more by male rather than female viewers. From start to finish it made no sense to me.

Around 9.15pm once more I made my way to Blue Coral although, once there, it was someone else and not Siba sitting out front. Clearly a comedian, because when I asked was Siba there he said with a straight face, 'He's gone home.'

Always assuming people tell the truth, I felt quite disappointed but just then someone shot out of the darkness from behind me. It was Siba, who grabbed my hand and led me to a seat on the porch. He still had on his working gear: a tee shirt and diving shorts. By now the other guy was busy nearby filling tanks with air. I assumed that was what they both had been doing before I arrived and so I said I would go if he was busy.

He said he didn't want me to go but nevertheless he did seem pre-occupied. I asked was everything O.K. and he admitted that it was because of his results in the test earlier in the day. His answers to two of the questions had been wrong.

A little later, when he showed me the test paper it turned out that there were many 'big words' that he didn't understand, which only compounded the problem. He was quite despondent by now, as I imagined it only served to confirm what he had in fact suspected: that there was no way he would be ready by October to take the exam. I went through the questions and explained a lot of the words to him. He asked could we do some more the following night after work and so I agreed to meet him there at 9.00pm. As it was we were there scrutinising the papers until 1.00am.

The following day was Sunday and, because of my late night 'teaching' session, I was later than usual into breakfast at 9.00am. As I was finishing around 10.00am I heard the sound of music and drums. The sounds got louder and louder and I realised it was a parade of some sorts. I rushed to get my camera and went outside to investigate.

A long crocodile of people: children in traditional costume and young men and women too, all marching to the sound of Kecimol, the traditional music of Lombok. The main position was held by the drummer. He was sitting high on what looked like a wagon, which was being pulled by some of the men. I decided I would walk along with them and take some photographs. One of the men stepped out of the procession and asked did I want him to take a photograph of me walking in the procession. I handed him my camera, he took the shot and then whipped round the other side and took one of a little girl who, moments later, he later explained was his daughter. I asked did he want me to send him the photograph. He told me no, it was O.K. He just wanted me to have a picture of her, which I thought was a lovely gesture. I completed the circuit of the village with them, everyone happy and smiling. It was impossible not to be drawn into the positive atmosphere.

Walking back past Coral Diving I saw Siba at the edge of the sea teaching some diving students. I stopped for a couple of minutes, but not surprisingly, he was so engrossed in what he was doing, he didn't even look up.

That afternoon, emboldened by my earlier snorkelling lesson, I hired a mask and fins as I walked to the beach. But once there, the idea of actually putting on the fins and attempting to walk into the sea with them on, was ridiculous, especially given my lack of experience. Carrying the mask into the sea was far less obvious but, once in there I realised as I waded further out that the current was quite strong. I was actually afraid of drifting too far out.

Back on the beach I spotted Siba twice more: once, sitting on the back of the Coral diving boat presumably going out to a dive and, two hours later, perched right at the front of the boat on their return. It was evident that, unlike myself, he was totally at home on the sea.

I arrived back at 4.30pm, showered and changed and went out to eat at 7.00pm. The restaurant was showing Philadelphia. As with most of the movies shown in these restaurants, I had seen it before, but anything starring Tom Hanks I can always watch again.

At 9.20 I wandered up to the diving school to meet Siba, who still had to shower and change. As I waited, a German diving instructor turned up with a bottle of Pernod and proceeded to hand round Pernod and cake to everyone. Then Siba showed up and asked did we want to go to a party. It was only a few doors down at one of the restaurants where there was music and dancing. We soon found a seat, I bought a couple of beers for us and asked Siba did he dance. He said he did but 'Not yet!' Little did he know how familiar that sounded to me, growing up in an era where most of the men preferred to stand at the edge of the dancefloor and watch rather than get down on it. I then asked him if any of his friends danced and he said, 'No!'

Hmm, I thought.

However, much to my delight, very soon Tom was up dancing and so I joined him, while Siba sat and watched. A little later an Australian couple, both Siba's students, sat next to us and chatted for a while. The man, Gary, told me that Siba was a very good teacher. I imagined he would be. He was clearly so dedicated and passionate about what he does. I got up a few times to dance with Tom and their other friend, who appeared to excel at a kind of Lambada, Indonesian style. Half way through the evening Siba disappeared and was away for about twenty minutes. I wondered if constant observer status had become too much to bear but, when he returned, he revealed he had an upset stomach.

We left soon after that and he walked me back to where I was staying. He confessed he was jealous and that was because he cared for me. He then said, 'Now I am going home to the bed. I want you to go home to the bed now. I don't want you to go back to the party!' Normally, I might just bristle at such control thinly disguised as a compliment. But I had had a pretty full day and by then it was 2.00am. I didn't put it into so many words, only smiled in response. But after dancing throughout the evening, I reckoned I probably had just enough energy to walk to my room, clean my teeth, get into bed and fall asleep. Besides I knew I had an early start the following day.

I was up at 6.30am, had breakfast by 7.00 and then set off, arriving at the area of the beach that served as a 'harbour' half an hour later. The sun was incredibly hot even then. The public ferry sailed at 8.15am. On the small boat I sat next to an old man wearing a battered hat with a brim. At one point he lifted his head, looked up at the sun and then turned to me. 'Mata hari', he said in a gravelly voice. I was tired and it took a moment for the penny to drop, but I realised he was referring to the sun. I was later to learn that in the Indonesian language this translates as 'Eye of Dawn'. At the time I had only a vague recollection of a woman by that name with some kind of reputation as a spy. In fact, Mata Hari was the stage name of a Dutch exotic dancer and courtesan who was convicted of being a spy for Germany during World War 1. She was executed by firing squad in France.

When we arrived in Bangsal I had an hour to wait for the shuttle to Senggigi. I waited in the restaurant and met the two Dutch guys I encountered on the journey over. Then who should walk in but Hendrich. Since travelling with him on the bus from Yogyakarta I reckoned I had 'bumped into' him about six times. I really liked him as he was so easy to talk to. He was on his way to the airport to fly to Singapore for twelve days and then he was returning home. He confessed he was now ready to go back. He gave me his address and wished me well in Australia.

DISILLUSION IN SENGGIGI

The bus arrived in Senggigi around 11.30am. I looked up *The Hero*, which Siba had recommended. It was indeed very nice, but too expensive for my budget at 20,000R and so I went back to the Pantai Indah, where I got a very basic room for 10,000R. Just a square box housing a single bed, but it was clean and just a few steps to the shower. It would suit me for a couple of nights. I handed over my laundry at reception before returning and taking a shower. I was so tired by then I just fell into bed and slept until about 2.30pm, when I went out for a walk to re-orientate myself.

Siba had told me only that he might be back that afternoon around 5.00pm but it was far too early to eat and so I turned up at the restaurant around 7.30pm. There was no sign of him and one of the waiters hadn't heard from him. I told him I wanted to see Siba before I left but, for some reason, (no doubt too many late nights and early mornings) I got the days mixed up. I mistakenly thought it was 20th. I told him too that my birthday was the following day the 21st and so I would come to eat dinner in the restaurant tomorrow. Perhaps Siba would be back then I thought. He told me to write a note to Siba and he would give it to him as soon as he appeared and so that's what I did. I'm almost sure I dated the note 20th August and so it was quite likely that Siba would have realised my mistake. After dinner I left returning straight to my box of a room, read for a while and then fell asleep.

It was only when I started to write up my journal the following day after breakfast I realised my mistake with the dates. I felt very foolish. Hmm! Not for the first time in this trip I reminded myself, before adopting a kinder tone. *Travelling within different cultures is a big learning curve. Don't be so hard on yourself!*

So now I had a whole day for which I had made no plans. The truth was, I did not know quite what to do with it. I decided I would walk up to the Telecom Office and send a fax to Paul, even though I knew it would be the middle of the night where he was. I eventually found the place but, as luck would have it, their fax was broken. Ah, well. Perhaps it wasn't such a good idea after all.

I found the nearest beach restaurant and ordered a Coke. Trying to engage my sensible brain, I attempted to work out my plan for the next week and also to figure out how much it might cost me. Always essential. By the time I returned to the hotel about noon I was feeling quite miserable. I decided I would write Siba a letter and take it with me to the restaurant that evening, simply because I didn't believe he would be there. I had no heart then to do anything else but read for the remainder of the afternoon.

At 5.20pm there was a loud knock on the door. I asked who it was and a deep voice shouted, 'Siba'. I couldn't believe it and my first thought was, typically, I must look such a mess, having been in the stuffy atmosphere of this tiny room all afternoon. I opened the door and he was leaning against the window, absolutely wet through. He told me he had just returned from Trewangan and it had been raining. I told him how sad I had been feeling as I imagined I wouldn't see him before I left. 'Why would you think that,' was his response. I just smiled, thinking that moment was neither the time nor the place to reveal my deep-seated insecurities in the 'emotional department.' He told me he had been given my message and asked did I want to eat at the Blue Coral that evening as he would be there.

I arrived around 7.30pm. The waiter I had met before came straight up to me and asked my name. He told me he had given my special message to Siba and that he was there earlier but had a phone call and had to go home. I ordered a Coke, he brought some popcorn and then wished me 'Happy Birthday, which was when I had to admit to him that I had mixed up the dates and it wasn't actually until the following day. Clearly an optimist, he just laughed and said that was good as I could now celebrate it two nights running now.

Just then Siba appeared looking quite lovely in jeans and a white shirt. He sat opposite me and we were joined by another of his friends, Agus, whose birthday was the 23rd. August. The restaurant was not busy at all. Next, the owner, Siba's boss, appeared and introduced himself. He was from Taiwan but had been in Lombok for five years. He had no English and so, as he spoke, Siba acted as interpreter. I quickly learned his whole conversation was clearly a practised lesson in unashamedly fulsome, but not necessarily sincere, flattery.

My dark colouring (now with touches of grey) was more French or Italian looking than English. My hairstyle and profile was like Lady Di's. That I was very beautiful and no doubt my mother was too. That I had a much nicer smile than any other English person he knew. At that moment he reached for my hand, turned it over to peer at my palm and said something (Siba muttered something at this point) about me having many lovers. He said I was not emotional. When I challenged that one, he recanted by saying I easily forgave people. He told me I was intellectual that I thought deeply about things, that I find it hard to keep money and that I had a lot of energy. I glanced at Siba at one point as his translation never faltered. However, he was clearly good at multi-tasking as throughout the whole translation, he was completing an application form.

After I had finished my meal I bought a beer to share with Siba. He sat and talked some more about his relationship with the other instructors. They sounded to me like a lazy, irresponsible lot. I knew in the very short time I had known Siba, that he, for one, was not either of those. He said he was always having to take in things they left lying around outside, sometimes clothing, sometimes valuable equipment. He told me that one of them in particular had a habit of leaving money lying around outside for days. When he then could not locate it, he would accuse one of the local boys of stealing. Then the boss would kick the boy out. Siba believed this was a deliberate ploy when they wanted to get rid of one of them. Quite often Siba would be the one left to lock up, as the others would tend to say they weren't able to do it. He appeared to me to be caught in the middle and shouldering far too much responsibility.

As the evening wore on, he admitted he was tired and so asked did I want to meet him tomorrow to celebrate my actual birthday. Well of course I did, as it would be my last night in Lombok. We arranged to meet in the *Sunshine Restaurant* the following evening. How appropriate for a Leo birthday I thought to myself. In this case though, I was to discover that, just like Pride, Optimism also Comes Before a Fall.

Happy Birthday to me! And it was actually the 21st this time. I had checked in my diary just to be sure. After breakfast, I set off to find the bank at Chakanegara. It was very straightforward with the help of Siba's written directions and so, after withdrawing some money, I returned to Senggigi. By then it was hot and I was full of restless energy and so I decided the only place to be was on the beach, where I swam for quite some time before relaxing in the sunshine.

I returned to my little room around 4.00pm, took a shower then lay down for a while, before getting changed to go out to the *Sunshine Restaurant* to meet Siba. The image I had conjured up was of a small restaurant overlooking the beach, where we would enjoy a last meal together before I had to leave. Ah, what a hopeless deluded Romantic!

I arrived at *Sunshine Restaurant* at just turned 7.30pm and was amused by someone telling me my friend was waiting for me upstairs. I looked up, only to see Siba leaning over a balustrade. He waved and then disappeared from view.

I climbed the stairs and entered the room, which was about as far from the image of my vision as it was possible to be. It was a large, fairly empty, featureless room, with a couple of big round tables. At one of the tables sat Siba with a friend, who I thought would perhaps leave as I'd arrived. In front of each of them sat a pint of beer. I ordered a coke. We exchanged a few pleasantries which, in the circumstances felt a little awkward. About half an hour later, Siba left the room, saying he would be back shortly. Another disappearing act I thought!

A moment later his friend, gesturing to the balcony, asked quite innocently who Siba was with. Clearly designed to get me to go to look, which I did, it seemed he was quite enjoying the situation.

When I peered over the balcony Siba was talking to an Indonesian woman who, soon after came upstairs with him. Accompanying him was another woman with a small child. Curiouser and curiouser! I wasn't introduced. They talked together in Indonesian for a few minutes and then Siba turned to me to tell me that she had just flown in from Holland today. Then he added that her husband was a Dutch guy.

The atmosphere was clearly strained but I tried to make conversation. It stopped however at the point where I asked what her husband did? The woman, Kutut, who I learned later was originally from Bali, was clearly getting more and more angry with Siba in response to constant comments from the other guy, which of course I could not understand, although I could hazard a guess at the subject matter. The other woman with her seemed only to be able to giggle and simper.

At first, I thought how nice it was that Siba had asked his friends to join us, a little like a birthday party for me. But having a brain underneath all the 'romantic' mush, I was aware from the woman's body language that, married or not, her relationship with Siba was, or had been, clearly more complicated than just 'friends'.

By this time, I was beginning to feel as if I had been drawn, as a reluctant actor, into the middle of a weird kind of farce. I suppose, in the true sense of unwittingly, I had. Siba then exited the stage with the two women, leaving me once more with his 'friend', the true villain of the piece, who by now was definitely not one of my 'favourite' people. The moment Siba left the room he appeared to take pleasure in disparaging him. As if I couldn't have worked it out for myself.

When Siba returned, he told me she had phoned him to say she would be arriving that day and he had told them where he would be. Simple! I was really mad and challenged him, not about having girlfriends, past or present, but about allowing me both to be exposed to such an unpleasant atmosphere, not to mention his 'so-called' friend's unnecessary comments.

I should have known better than to have imagined he would handle *my* anger any better than he appeared to have handled hers. His defence? That I just didn't understand Eastern culture! I told him that was where he was very wrong. I understood it only too well. I just didn't want it to touch my life in this particular way.

I said I had seen enough and I was going. He still seemed to think I would want to write to him and so reminded me I could leave my address in the office tomorrow. I said emphatically, 'No!' He shrugged, said he knew I was angry with him and he was sorry for what had happened. I just turned, leaving both Siba and the *Sunshine Hotel*, the scene of my latest life lesson, behind me. I was angry, sad, disappointed and feeling very, very gullible and naïve. What a birthday! It would be one I certainly would not forget.

A BRIEF RETURN TO UBUD

The following day, on the bus to Ubud, I hunkered down in my seat unable to dispel the miserable feeling which accompanied me as I woke that morning. But, as with many travelling encounters, a change of scene will often offer up a change in circumstances and accompanying mood. I was soon chatting to Richard, a guy from Leeds. He had been diving with Blue Coral in Gili Air. Recounting his enjoyment of the dives lightened the atmosphere and I was soon feeling much better.

I arrived back at *Lastri House* about 3.00pm to be given my old room. It was lovely, a little like coming home. I went straight to *Casa Luna* for a salad sandwich, which was delicious and then returned to my room for a rest. At 7.00pm I went out to eat and called in at the Wartel to fax Paul and was delighted to have received a fax from Steph. I sent mine to them both and then returned to *Lastri House*. I was exhausted, no doubt because of the recent emotional turmoil, and so by 9.45pm I was in bed and straight to sleep.

I had breakfasted by 9.00am on one of Wayan's delicious banana concoctions. I went straight out afterwards to the bank to draw out some Australian dollars. I also swapped my book and went straight on to get my photographs developed. There was a lovely one of Rush with me and also a couple of Tara in Nepal.

The following day was one of practicalities, in preparation for the next stage of my journey. I spent the afternoon doing some clothes washing and decided to brighten up my daypack with a wash. After three months in South-east Asia it had developed another coating entirely. I decided I would write to Siba and so drafted out what I wanted to say. I didn't expect a reply, but needed typically for my own sake, to put my thoughts and feelings into words. I felt much better afterwards. Next, I called in at the fax office and again was happy to have received a couple: one from Paul (sent just before I'd sent mine to him yesterday) and one from Bex telling me her G.C.S.E. results.

I went out to eat at 6.30pm, but there were still queues at *Casa Luna* and so I opted for a tempe curry at *Benjis*. It was delicious. After eating I wrote out my letter to Siba there, before returning home, in bed for 10.30pm. I read a little of my novel and, once more, slept well.

After breakfast the following day, I called into the Perama office to confirm my seat to Kuta tomorrow, 25th August. On the way back, I bought a couple of sarongs, one for Paul and one for Julie, sorted out everything I would be sending home and then took it to the Post Office for packing. It weighed 4½ kgs which was not too bad at all. I sent back my tapes, the photographs, my Batik mask and the fabric, the Kopi hat, three sarongs and a wooden figure for Tom. Altogether, it came to 63,200 rupiah. With a great sense of completion, I returned at 1.00 pm, wrote up my journal and rested a while.

I was aware this was my last day in Ubud, I place I had come to love. Of course, I went out to eat at my favourite place, *Casa Luna*, but felt a little lonely sitting there on my own. I was more than happy with my own company during the day, but the evenings were always brightened by sharing. As if my inner musings had been heard, who should I bump into on the way back, but Charyn and Pete, friends I had made in Bukit Lawang. It was so good to see them. They had not eaten and so I joined them and Charyn's brother, but just had a drink whilst they ate. We chatted until about 11.00pm, swapping our stories since we had last met. It was the perfect way to spend my last night in Ubud.

KUTA

My last gorgeous breakfast assembled by Wayan and then I was settled on the Perama shuttle by 8.15am and on my way back to Kuta. It was a straightforward transfer, dropped off at *Poppies* and found no problem at all in getting a room at *Kedin's Inn*. At only 12,000R it was clean and reasonable and so I was very happy.

I changed and headed straight for the Post Office to pick up my mail. There were cards and letters from Tara, David, Michael, Diane, Valerie and Julie. I went for a drink and a bite to eat, while in time honoured fashion I read them over and over again. I still found that my heart sang to hear from everyone at home as well as people I had met whilst travelling.

That afternoon, I witnessed a mini drama whilst on the beach for an hour or so. A young local boy was carried unconscious from the sea. He was carried off the beach on a stretcher and later I learnt that, thankfully, he had been revived and was O.K.

I ate in *Kedin's* restaurant that evening and chatted to a couple of English girls. They asked did I want to meet them the following night as they were planning a night 'on the town'. We'll see! I'm not sure I'm in the mood. Since leaving Lovina beach I've been experiencing a restlessness. Even time spent with Siba on Trewangan didn't dispel it altogether. I remember telling him back in Senggigi that I had become bored with sitting or lying around on beaches, although whether I am ready to return to work just yet I'm not so sure.

In that mood of missing the closeness of others, I was rather over optimistic in a second visit to the Post Office to check if there was any more mail. Nada! I drew out some more money and then wandered around in an attempt to locate a Garuda agent to reconfirm my flight to Sydney. Typically, having looked far and wide there was one just around the corner from Kedins.

Still unable to resist the beach I stole a couple of hours, before returning to my room to shower. Following what had become my usual pattern I then lay down for a doze and a read before going out to meet Shelley and Sara at 7.30pm.

We watched Babe, a film I actually love and then around 11.30pm we all went off to the *Sari Club*, the so-called 'happening' place in Kuta. We all downed a 'Down Under' cocktail – a seemingly lethal mix of Arak and fruit juice. We chatted to some Australians and then I found myself dancing with a weird Kiwi, who referred to everything as 'cool'. We all danced in a group together which was light-hearted and fun. I shared a complimentary remark with the girls about the moves of an Indonesian guy who was dancing nearby and they promptly dragged him over to join us. He looked a little embarrassed and I felt sorry for him. He told us he was Javanese, at university in Jakarta and on holiday in Bali. His English was not bad at all, although he said he would like to improve it.

By this time, I was feeling a bit 'squiffy' on the 'Down Unders' and realised it was 2.50am. We went shortly after, Shelley and Sara kindly escorting me home. I just keeled over on the bed and amazingly felt no ill effects.

When I awoke at 9.30am, I was feeling a little delicate to say the least. I read for most of the day and at 6.00pm went out on my own to the *Seaview Restaurant* and ordered a pizza. Afterwards, back at *Kedins* I enjoyed a quiet evening reading and was in bed by 9.30pm.

My very last day in Indonesia. I felt very sad about leaving the country and strangely had mixed feelings about going on to Australia, not least because of being aware of the tripling of the cost of living. I did some shopping: swapping my Indonesia book for a Rough Guide to Australia and then bought a lovely silver bangle and a postcard to send to Julie. Once more I called into the Post Office and was delighted to get a card from Margaret and a letter from Beryl. I decided I would pay for another night to give me time to relax later.

At lunch time I went to the *Tree House*. It wasn't very busy and the young waitress there, Made, talked a little about herself. She told me she often gets stressed because of lack of money and so I ended up giving her 40,000R, which I wouldn't get so much on exchanging in Oz. She gave me a big hug and said she would send me a photo of her wedding in September.

I had arranged for the guy from the hotel to take me to the airport for 10,000R, about 1,500 more than a taxi but no hassle and so everything was set to go. I went on the beach for the very last time, came back, showered and ate dinner early about 6.00pm at *Kedins Inn*. By the time I had packed everything it was still only 7.00pm. I decided to spend my remaining rupiah on a phone call home. I went to a Wartel on the front and luckily caught Paul in. It was good to speak with him just before I left.

I was still feeling pretty unsettled about moving on. It seemed a big step to take at this next stage of my journey and, of course, another big change in culture. From the relatively relaxed atmosphere of south-east Asia back into the possibly full-on, stressful vibes of a city. I doubted my ability to cope with it.

It was 8.30pm when I was dropped off at the airport. I went straight to check-in and who should I meet but Ted, Rob and Karen's friend. He had just been in Australia and had spent the day in Bali in transit. We sat at the bar, had a drink and chatted for about an hour and a half. After he left me I made my way to the Gate for my plane. It brought back memories of setting off from Gatwick four and a half months ago – (was it only four and half months ago?) and having to say goodbye to Julie at the Gate. Another ending another beginning.

We got away on time at 11.10pm. Take off was smooth but the rest of the 5 ½ hour flight not so much. Whether it was down to stormy weather I didn't know but for at least 2 hours we experienced constant turbulence. I was not always one for signs and portents but, during this time on the flight, it crossed my mind more than once, whether this could possibly be a sign of things to come.

ACKNOWLEDGEMENTS

This book is based on my journal, a small, soft-backed book given to me as a present before I left for my own Distant Blue Horizons.

I had moved house many times in my life but, back then at the end of 1995, when I was contemplating one of the biggest 'moves' I had ever made: selling my house and leaving Dorset, a place I loved, to strike out into the world, I was advised by an astrologer not to make the trip 'purposeless.'

I suppose then for me my 'purpose' was to document as much as possible of the experience and that was where my journal came in.

It fitted easily into my backpack, which was my 'home' for the whole twelve months I was away. Carrying your 'home' on your back in this way makes you appreciate what possessions you really need. What you truly value and why.

I had not been away for very long before I realised that my journal was my most treasured possession. As someone travelling alone, although I met many other people, there were also times when I was very much *on my own*. My journal was, among other things, my travel companion. And, as the journey continued, it was to become the one thing I knew I could not bear to lose.

So too, while I was away, much as I lived the experience to the full and made many close connections, I was aware of needing regular contact with the people I loved back home. In the days before mobile phones, connecting from the other side of the world, meant it was always the written word in the form of letters, cards or faxes that served to keep me in touch with family and friends.

My thanks and love especially to Julie, who was my inspiration and support at the beginning of the trip and to Paul, who stored my few belongings whilst I was away and drove all the way from Cumbria to Gatwick to welcome me back at the end. And not forgetting Tom who adopted my little cat Phoebe.

I hope too that the written words in these pages will bring you as much pleasure as the journey they relate held for me.

On a more sombre note, I am aware that in recent years there have been disasters: earthquakes in Nepal and floods in Thailand and Indonesia.

My thoughts have been for those lovely people, who I was

privileged to call my friends whilst I was away. I pray that they are all safe.

A NOTE FROM THE AUTHOR

I hope you have enjoyed journeying with me through Southeast Asia in the pages of this book.

I have lived my trip again in the writing of it, as memories of the people I met, the countries I travelled through and the places I stayed, came flooding back.

I am aware that striking out to travel alone around the world, although initially daunting, seemed then to hold less of a threat than it may do in the present day.

Sadly, the world and many of the countries within it, appear now to be experiencing more extreme views and much division.

To the contrary, all those years ago, what I encountered and valued on my journey was a strong sense of connection with people from all over the world. A recognition that, beneath the layers of parental, cultural and societal conditioning, beneath the skin, we are all the same: human beings with a need for love, warmth, understanding and connection.

A REQUEST

If you have enjoyed this book and have a moment to spare, I would appreciate it if you could write a short review on the Amazon page where you bought it. Reviews make a massive difference in helping new readers to find the books.

Thank you.

Susanne

AN EXTRACT FROM THE NEXT STAGE IN THE JOURNEY

AUSTRALIA

SYDNEY

Arriving over Australia there was a glorious red sunrise. We landed at 6.45am and of course the first thing that struck me, after the balmy Bali temperature, was the freezing cold. Thank God I decided to keep my Polar Tec jacket, which I'd only really worn on the trek. I certainly needed it now.

While waiting for the bus to Glebe and the *Hereford Street Hostel* I sat with Anna, a Swedish girl and Volke, a German guy, who were also going to the hostel. Anna and I agreed to share a room. It cost $22 dollars for me as a YHA (Youth Hostel Association). member. We were shown to our room and Anna went straight to bed and fell asleep. But for me, no matter how I tried, sleep just would not come. Untrammelled thoughts soon led to rising feeling of panic and anxiety.

The following morning, I decided I would do my usual trip to check my post and so started walking into town. There was a letter and a card but with my burgeoning negative thoughts, it seemed it was not enough for me and could only feel disappointment about the people I had not heard from. I felt so totally alone and without any motivation or energy to look for work, which would have to be 'sous la table' as I was much too old to possess a work permit. I knew many people did it but what hope did I have, without connections, in finding what I needed.

When I returned to the hostel Anna was still peacefully sleeping. In a state of desperation, feeling really bad, sick and extremely tired I went straight back out to STA Travel and asked about going home immediately. The woman in the agency would be able to arrange half of the itinerary she told me, but there was a problem on the Chicago part of the American Airlines ticket. I said I would call in tomorrow at 11.00am to complete the arrangements.

Back at the hostel I told Anna that I was going and I could see immediately that she was shocked at my decision. I also rang Lianne and arranged to see her in a couple of days on the Saturday. She told me she didn't live too far away from Glebe and so she offered to come and pick me up at 10.30am. I had a big plate of fish and chips for my tea and then went up to the room to read. Anna had gone out by then and so I was on my own. As I lay there feeling very cold in the narrow bed, too tired to think over much, it was impossible to believe that only two nights before I had been in tropical temperatures.

I woke around 8.00am, but was still exhausted and so carried on dozing for a while until Anna came in at 9.15am. I knew we had to check out by 10.00am as Anna was leaving and so I would need to check into another room. I quickly washed and dressed and we both went down to breakfast together.

As we chatted, restored by a good night's sleep, I began to realise I had acted too impulsively. I was vaguely aware that a pattern of mine, when backed into a corner, especially when feeling hurt, lost or alone had always tended to be simply to run, escape, get away anywhere.

No doubt chatting to Anna, but mainly the contact with Lianne, who I knew I could trust, made most of the difference, allowing me to begin to see through a more positive lens. I told myself that even though things may very well be difficult in that moment, I should at least give it more time. Anything could happen to change things. That would be my mantra. And, ultimately, even if it did not work out I could still go home knowing that at least I had given it the best go I possibly could.

Printed in Great Britain
by Amazon

15927084R00185